John Stevens

Englisch einfach richtig

TYPISCHE FEHLER VERMEIDEN

Hueber Verlag

Zeichnungen: Irmtraud Guhe, München

3. 2. 1. | Die letzten Ziffern
2023 22 21 20 19 | bezeichnen Zahl und Jahr des Druckes.
Alle Drucke dieser Auflage können, da unverändert, nebeneinander benutzt werden.
1. Auflage

Basiert auf ISBN 978-3-19-357918-8
Umschlaggestaltung: Sieveking · Agentur für Kommunikation, München
Umschlagfoto: © Getty Images Plus/iStock/stockfour
Layout und Satz: Sieveking · Agentur für Kommunikation, München
Verlagsredaktion: Helga Aichele, Hueber Verlag, München
Druck und Bindung: Firmengruppe APPL, aprinta druck GmbH, Wemding
Printed in Germany
ISBN 978-3-19-017918-3

Art. 530_26429_001_01

Vorwort

Für wen ist dieses Buch
Sie sprechen bereits Englisch, aber es schleichen sich immer wieder dieselben Fehler ein? Sie sind sich z. B. manchmal nicht sicher, ob Sie die richtige Zeitform oder das richtige Wort gewählt haben? Zwei Formen sind sich ähnlich und Sie wissen nicht, für welche Sie sich entscheiden sollen? Kurzum: Sie möchten Ihr Englisch verbessern und die typischen Fehler verlernen? Dann ist dieses Buch genau das Richtige für Sie.

Was Sie mit diesem Buch erreichen können
Mit diesem Übungsbuch können Sie gezielt Ihr Englisch von lästigen Fehlern befreien, zu denen deutschsprachige Lernende immer wieder neigen. *Englisch einfach richtig* bietet Ihnen rund 290 Übungen zu Grammatik, Wortschatz und Sprachgebrauch und ist bestens zum praktischen und schnellen Wiederholen und Üben geeignet.

Wie das Buch aufgebaut ist
Englisch einfach richtig besteht aus zwei Teilen: *Common Mistakes in English Grammar* und *True and False Friends*. Im Inhaltsverzeichnis finden Sie hierzu detailliertere Informationen. Selbstverständlich enthält das Buch im Anhang auch einen Lösungsschlüssel, mit dem Sie Ihre Arbeit kontrollieren und notfalls berichtigen können. Hier finden Sie auch ergänzende Erklärungen zu den typischen Fehlern – jeweils nach diesem Symbol ▶. Am Ende des Buches befindet sich außerdem ein alphabetisches Register, das ein schnelles Auffinden der behandelten Wörter und Themen ermöglicht.

Wie Sie mit dem Buch arbeiten können
Suchen Sie die Themen, die Sie gezielt üben möchten, oder bearbeiten Sie systematisch ein Kapitel nach dem anderen. Die Übungen sind kurz und abwechslungsreich, so dass Sie entsprechend Ihrer Zeiteinteilung üben können.

Jedes Thema bietet Übungen unterschiedlichen Schwierigkeitsgrades (von Niveau A2 bis B2 des *Gemeinsamen Europäischen Referenzrahmens*). Das Symbol ⚡ direkt neben der Übungsziffer kennzeichnet Übungen auf dem Niveau B2. Wollen Sie gezielt auf dem Niveau B2 üben, konzentrieren Sie sich auf diese Übungen.

Übung macht den Meister!
Lassen Sie sich nicht entmutigen, wenn Sie eine Übung nicht auf Anhieb richtig lösen können. Es ist geradezu der Zweck mancher Übungen, Aha-Erlebnisse auszulösen und somit ein besseres Verständnis für die Strukturen der englischen Sprache zu ermöglichen. Am besten Sie wiederholen die Übung zu einem späteren Zeitpunkt und lernen einfach dazu – ganz nach dem Motto *Practice makes perfect!* (Übung macht den Meister!)

Viel Spaß und viel Erfolg
Autor und Verlag

Inhaltsverzeichnis

Grammatik – Common Mistakes in English Grammar

Wortschatz und Sprachgebrauch – True and False Friends

Grammatik – Common Mistakes in English Grammar

1. Einfache Form und Verlaufsform

1. I'm just finishing my lunch.
2. I live in Hameln.
3. A phone call
4. *Have* and *having*
5. They aren't taking a holiday this year.
6. I don't like the sound of all this.
7. Trends
8. It seems very cold.
9. I was still having breakfast.
10. I need a drink.

1

1 I'm just finishing my lunch.

Was passt zusammen?

1. I'm
2. Isabella
3. Why do
4. Ronald
5. Does
6. The boss says
7. The train
8. Do

a. he doesn't like the idea.
b. Mike still live in Merrow?
c. is working from home today.
d. they always arrive late?
e. doesn't run on Saturdays.
f. you really believe that?
g. just finishing my lunch.
h. works only part-time. She has kids.

1	2	3	4	5	6	7	8
g							

2 I live in Hameln.

Unterstreichen Sie die richtige Form.

1. I (a.) am living / (b.) live in Hameln. I've lived there all my life.
2. A friend of ours from Canada (a.) is staying / (b.) stays with us at the moment.
3. ◆ (a.) Are you enjoying / (b.) Do you enjoy the party?
   ● Yes, thanks. I (c.) am having / (d.) have a great time.
4. (a.) I am not having / (b.) I don't have lunch in the canteen usually. I nearly always (c.) am bringing / (d.) bring something to eat from home.
5. Jackie (a.) has / (b.) is having a part-time job in a lawyer's office. But she's going to have a baby soon.
6. People (a.) aren't wanting / (b.) don't want to hear bad news. That's why politicians (c.) promise / (d.) are promising heaven on earth.

3 A phone call

Ergänzen Sie. Zwei Ausdrücke werden nicht benötigt.

arrives • I can see • I don't think so • ~~I'm just walking~~
is just arriving • is shining • It snows • It's snowing • seem

◆ Where are you? Are you at the station yet?
● Yes, (1.) *I'm just walking* into the station building now.
◆ You're late, aren't you?
● (2.) ______. It's 9.47, and their train is due at 9.49. It might be late because of the weather anyway. (3.) ______ hard here at the moment.
◆ The sun (4.) ______ here.
● OK, I'm at the arrivals and departures board. A lot of people (5.) ______ to be waiting. There are quite a few delays posted, but Ann & Ian's train is on time. Platform 5. Oh, (6.) ______ it now. The train (7.) ______.

4 *Have and having*

Ergänzen Sie *I have* oder *I'm having*.

1. Sorry, *I have* no time this weekend.
2. ______ an argument with my internet provider on the other line. I'll call you back.
3. ______ lunch with Diana next Tuesday.
4. ______ a really great holiday. The hotel, the beach, the people – all just great.
5. ______ a party on 10th May. Can you come?
6. ______ a lot to do this morning.
7. ______ three children, two boys and a girl.

5 They aren't taking a holiday this year.

Sortieren Sie die Teile und bilden Sie Sätze. Achtung: Nicht alle Teile werden benötigt!

1. a holiday / aren't taking / don't take / they / this year
   They aren't taking a holiday this year.
2. does / is / mean / meaning / this symbol / what
   ____
3. Joanna / to lose / is trying / some weight / tries
   ____
4. doesn't eat / isn't eating / meat / she
   Ann's a vegetarian. ______________________________
5. is just closing / just closes / the tourist office
   ____
6. closes / earlier / is closing / it / in the winter
   ____
7. gets better / slowly / is getting better / the situation
   ____
8. am not / I / remember / don't / anything / remembering
   ____

6 I don't like the sound of all this.

Ergänzen Sie die richtige Gegenwartsform.

1. I (not / like) _don't like_ the sound of all this.
2. We (not / know) ____________________ why he did it.
3. Ron and Claire (not / speak) ____________________ to each other at the moment.
4. Jem (make) ____________________ real progress.
5. We (need) ____________________ more time.
6. The paperback version (not / cost) ____________________ so much.
7. I (not / mind) ____________________ what you do.
8. ◆ What (you / do) ____________________?
   ● I (try) ____________________ to repair this door handle.
9. Jan and Ed have split up. Ed (live) ____________________ temporarily with me.
10. Temperatures (rise) ____________________ worldwide.
11. Who (you / wait) ____________________ for?
12. What (this word / mean) ____________________?

7 Trends

Korrigieren Sie.

1. People ~~go~~ *are going* on shorter holidays.
2. Winters ~~become~~ ______________ warmer and wetter in many parts of the globe.
3. The price of oil ~~rises~~ ______________ again.
4. More fathers ~~take~~ ______________ time off to care for their children.
5. People ~~worry~~ ______________ about the economy more.
6. Employers ~~give~~ ______________ more short-term contracts.
7. People ~~buy~~ ______________ smaller cars that use less fuel.
8. More and more people ~~live~~ ______________ a second life online.

8 It seems very cold.

Korrigieren Sie.

1. It ~~is seeming~~ *seems* very cold. Is the heating not on?
2. ~~Are you remembering~~ ______________ what happened?
3. She's very rich. She ~~is owning~~ ______________ six hotels.
4. No, this ~~isn't belonging~~ ______________ to me.
5. I ~~am not seeing~~ ______________ what you are trying to say.
6. ~~Were you understanding~~ ______________ what he just said?

9 I was still having breakfast.

Korrigieren Sie – falls nötig.

1. They fixed a fault in the computer system so I couldn't work.
   They were fixing a fault in the computer system so I couldn't work.
2. We didn't eat till they arrived.
   We ______________________ till they ________________.
3. We still sat at the table at midnight.
   We ______________________ at the table at midnight.
4. We saw a flash of light, then we heard a loud explosion.
   We ____________ a flash of light, then we ____________ a loud explosion.
5. I listened to music and had headphones on, so I didn't hear anything.
   I ____________ to music and ____________ headphones on, so I ____________ anything.
6. The boss walked in when we discussed his new hairstyle.
   The boss ____________ when we ______________ his new hairstyle.
7. It rained hard, so I decided to take a taxi.
   It ____________ hard, so I ____________ to take a taxi.
8. I still had breakfast when the taxi arrived.
   I ______________________ breakfast when the taxi ____________.

10 I need a drink.

Übersetzen Sie.

1. Ich brauche etwas zu trinken.
   I need a drink.
2. Es hängt alles davon ab *(depend)*, was es kostet.
3. Ich arbeite zurzeit von zu Hause.
4. Ich lerne Spanisch.
5. Als ich hinkam *(arrive)*, warteten schon über 50 Menschen.
6. Sie bauen ein neues Hotel.
7. Normalerweise stehe ich samstags später auf.
8. Aber heute arbeite ich.

2. Present Perfect und Vergangenheit

11. I've seen the report.
12. A or B?
13. We went to Amsterdam last weekend.
14. I've seen this film.
15. I've never eaten kangaroo.
16. When did this come?
17. An email
18. Delaying tactics
19. Have you ever ...?
20. Finders, keepers

11 I've seen the report.

Was passt zusammen?

1. I've
2. I read it
3. Have you
4. The plane has just
5. It
6. We
7. Has
8. Have there

a. met Jack?
b. been any phone calls?
c. anything important happened?
d. last week.
e. left London late.
f. seen the report.
g. landed.
h. were both at the Frankfurt conference.

1	2	3	4	5	6	7	8
f							

12 A or B?

Was passt: a oder b?

1. The meeting has just (a.) began / (b.) begun.
2. I've never (a.) fell / (b.) felt so good.
3. We (a.) flew / (b.) flown to Chicago, not New York.
4. I've completely (a.) forgot / (b.) forgotten.
5. She's (a.) spend / (b.) spent quite a lot of time in China.
6. We (a.) swam / (b.) swum out to an island.
7. Who (a.) laid / (b.) lay the table?
8. I (a.) laid / (b.) lay down, but I couldn't sleep.

1	2	3	4	5	6	7	8
b							

13 We went to Amsterdam last weekend.

Streichen Sie den falschen Satz durch.

1. Wir sind letztes Wochenende nach Amsterdam gefahren.
   a. ~~We have been to Amsterdam last weekend.~~
   b. We went to Amsterdam last weekend.

2. Wir waren noch nie vorher dort.
   a. We've never been there before.
   b. We were never there before.

3. Wir waren schon einmal in Den Haag.
   a. We've been to Den Haag before.
   b. We were in Den Haag before.

4. Wir haben auf einem Hausboot gewohnt.
   a. We've stayed in a houseboat.
   b. We stayed in a houseboat.

5. Es war wunderschön.
   a. It's been wonderful.
   b. It was wonderful.

6. Wir haben viel gesehen und hatten viel Spaß.
   a. We saw a lot and had a great time.
   b. We've seen a lot and had a great time.

7. Wir sind in diesem Frühjahr bisher schon zwei Mal verreist.
   a. We've been away twice so far this spring.
   b. We were away twice so far this spring.

14 I've seen this film.

Ergänzen Sie wie im Beispiel.

1. I've seen this film.
   I saw it last week with Hugh.
2. I've done this journey many times.
   ______________________ for the first time in 2005.
3. We've begun to pack.
   ____________________________ yesterday.
4. I've spoken to Jill.
   ______________________ to her on Monday.
5. I haven't slept very well.
   ______________________ only three hours last night.
6. Jack has shown the visitors round.
   ____________________________ when they arrived.
7. I've rung the embassy.
   ______________________ yesterday too.
8. I've paid the bill.
   ______________________ two days ago.
9. Someone has stolen my parking space.
   __________________________ on Tuesday too.

15 I've never eaten kangaroo.

Ergänzen Sie.

decided • didn't • didn't • ~~eaten~~ • had • have eaten
said • tasted • thought • was

Have you ever (1.) *eaten* kangaroo meat?
I (2.) ____________ some last month when I
(3.) ____________ on holiday in New South Wales.
It (4.) ____________ strange, and I (5.) ____________
really like it. But I (6.) ____________ want to hurt
my Australian hosts' feelings, so in true British
fashion I (7.) ____________ that I (8.) ____________ it
was "very interesting". I (9.) ____________ worse
things before, but I (10.) ____________ that next time someone offers me
some I will say no.

16 When did this come?

Ergänzen Sie.

- ◆ When (1. this / come) *did this come*?
- ● Someone (2. bring) ____________ it about ten minutes ago.
- ◆ Why (3. you / not open) ____________ it?
- ● Because it's addressed to you.
- ◆ But I (4. not order) ____________ anything from a company called Webspan.
- ● Maybe you (5. do) ____________, but you (6. forget) ____________.
- ◆ I (7. be) ____________ very busy lately, but I (8. not become) ____________ that forgetful!

17 An email

Ergänzen Sie Present Perfect, Vergangenheit oder Gegenwart.

Thank you for your suggestion. I (1. discuss) *have discussed* it with my colleagues and (2. be) ________________ pleased to tell you that we (3. decide) ________________ that we (4. think) ________________ it is a very good idea.
We have been partners for over 15 years now. During this time we (5. have) ________________ some difficult periods, especially since the credit crisis (6. break out) ________________ in late 2008. We (7. always look for) ________________ solutions that (8. serve) ________________ both parties, and feel that you (9. again find) ________________ one which is good for both of us.

18 Delaying tactics

Ergänzen Sie die passenden Verben im Present Perfect.

be • buy • check • ~~drink~~ • eat • give • give up • read

(1.) *I've drunk* two cups of coffee, (2.) ________________ my emails, and (3.) ________________ the latest news online, (4.) ________________ my plants some water, (5.) ________________ to the canteen and (6.) ________________ and (7.) ________________ a chocolate bar – (8.) ________________ smoking. So I suppose I'll have to start work now ...

19 Have you ever ...?

Ergänzen Sie die Fragen. Antworten Sie *Yes, I have* bzw. *No, I haven't.*

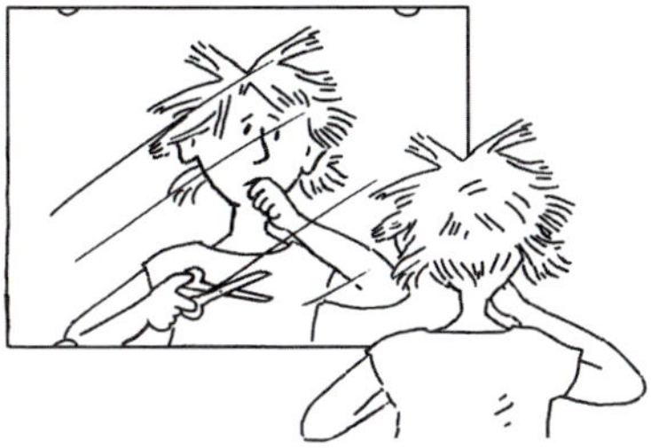

1. cut
   Have you ever cut your own hair? __________
2. drive
   __________ a sports car? __________
3. drink
   __________ real champagne? __________
4. ride
   __________ a camel? __________
5. buy
   __________ a diamond ring? __________
6. wear
   __________ a fur hat[1]? __________
7. sing
   __________ in a karaoke bar? __________
8. eat
   __________ seaweed[2]? __________

[1] Pelzmütze
[2] Seetang

20 Finders, keepers[1]

Ergänzen Sie.

(1. you / ever find) *Have you ever found* a large amount[2] of money in the street? I have. It (2. be) ______________ a few years ago, in a country that shall remain nameless[3], but which I (3. visit) ______________ many times in my life and which I (4. always love) ______________ very much. It (5. be) ______________ Eastertime, and we (6. be) ______________ there on a week's holiday. It (7. be) ______________ still cold at home, and we just (8. want) ______________ to get away from the long cold winter. I (9. often dream) ______________ of spending the winter in a warm southern country, but I (10. never have) ______________ the money, and I don't expect I ever will. Anyway, I (11. find) ______________ this 100 euro note in the street. I (12. not think) ______________ it was right to keep it, so I (13. take) ______________ it to the police. The first problem was that nobody (14. speak) ______________ English, and they (15. have to) ______________ go and find the local school teacher. I (16. explain) ______________ to her what had happened, and she (17. interpret[4]) ______________ for the policeman. He shrugged his shoulders[5] and (18. say) ______________ something I of course (19. not understand) ______________. The teacher (20. tell) ______________ me that the policeman (21. not want) ______________ any bother[6], and I should keep the money. That had never happened to me before, and (22. never happen) ______________ again since then!

[1] Wer's findet, dem gehört's
[2] große Menge
[3] das ungenannt bleiben soll
[4] dolmetschen
[5] zuckte mit den Schultern
[6] irgendwelche Scherereien

3. Present Perfect mit *since*, *for* und *how long*

21 *For or since?*

Kreuzen Sie an.

	since	for	
1.	X		2007
2.			two and a half years
3.			yesterday afternoon
4.			ten hours
5.			ten hours ago
6.			I don't know when
7.			ages
8.			sometime last year
9.			a short while
10.			a short while ago
11.			a long time
12.			as long as I can remember

22 What's right?

Kreuzen Sie an.

1. a. I have lived here for a long time.
   b. I have lived here since a long time.

2. a. How long do you know Mike?
   b. How long have you known Mike?

3. a. She hasn't been really fit ever since she had that accident.
   b. She isn't really fit ever since she had that accident.

4. a. I need some help, just for half an hour.
   b. I've needed some help, just for half an hour.

23 We're old friends.

Korrigieren Sie.

1. I ~~know~~ Jim since university.
   I have known Jim since university.
2. Mrs Franzen ~~is~~ ill ~~since~~ three weeks.
   Mrs Franzen ______________ ill ______________ three weeks.
3. How long ~~do~~ you ~~know~~ this?
   How long ______________________ this?
4. This situation ~~is developing since~~ a long time.
   This situation ______________________ a long time.
5. Things ~~calm down~~ since Watson ~~has left~~ the company.
   Things ______________ since Watson ______________ the company.
6. The company ~~is~~ active in Asia ~~since~~ over 30 years.
   The company ______________ active in Asia ______________ over 30 years.
7. How long ~~does~~ this problem ~~exist~~?
   How long ______________________?
8. How long ~~are you~~ with the company?
   How long ______________ with the company?

24 How long?

Ergänzen Sie die Fragen wie im Beispiel.

1. live
   How long have you been living here?
2. work
   ______________________________ for this company?
3. drive
   ______________________________ a car like that?
4. learn
   ______________________________ English?
5. wait
   ______________________________?
6. try
   ______________________________ to reach me?
7. sit
   ______________________________ there?
8. train
   ______________________________ for the marathon?
9. plan
   ______________________________ this?

4. Verneinung mit und ohne *do*

25 I'm not ready.

Was passt zusammen?

1. I'm not
2. I don't
3. I can't
4. I don't have
5. I didn't
6. I haven't
7. I hadn't

a. make Wednesday.
b. done this before.
c. expected to see William there.
d. meet anyone I knew.
e. agree.
f. to be at the meeting.
g. ready.

1	2	3	4	5	6	7
g						

26 A or B?

Was passt: a oder b?

1. We ... see them again for a long time.
   a) aren't going to b) don't
2. I ... much sport.
   a) don't b) don't do
3. I'm sorry, but I ... much English.
   a) don't speak b) speak not
4. You've misunderstood me. I ... that!
   a) meant not b) didn't mean

1	2	3	4

27 We're in a hurry.

Ergänzen Sie wie im Beispiel.

1. We're late.
   But we _aren't_ very late.
2. I know the first man.
   But I ______________ the other one.
3. We walked over twenty miles on the first day.
   But we ______________ so far on the next two.
4. I have plenty of time.
   But I ______________ much money!
5. I've made a mistake.
   I ______________ this kind of mistake for a long time.
6. I can speak a little Spanish.
   But I ______________ any Portuguese.
7. They'll give us something to drink.
   But they ______________ us anything to eat.
8. I do the washing.
   But I ______________ the ironing.

28 Why not?

Ergänzen Sie.

can't • didn't • don't • haven't • ~~isn't~~ • won't

1. Why *isn't* this stupid machine working?
2. Why ________ this stupid machine do what it's supposed to do?
3. Why ________ I spend a bit more money and buy something that was a bit more reliable?
4. Why ________ I just take it back to the shop and try and change it?
5. Why ________ they write instruction manuals that a normal person can understand?
6. Why ________ they updated the software?

29 Not a cold climate

Korrigieren Sie – falls nötig.

1. It's not a very wet climate.
   korrekt
2. It rains not often.
   ____
3. We have not many frosts.
   ____
4. You haven't to have a lot of thick coats.
   ____
5. We've not had snow for years.
   ____

30 No, that's not right.

Sortieren Sie die Teile und bilden Sie Sätze. Jeweils ein Wort wird nicht benötigt!

1. city / don't / I / in / live / not / the
   I don't live in the city.
2. before / ever / happened / hasn't / never / this
3. didn't / do / I / not / this
4. coming / don't / Frank / isn't / why / ?
5. decide / decided / didn't / till / we / yesterday
6. do / don't / making / more / preparation / why / you / ?
7. absolutely / agree / don't / I / not
8. doesn't / in / passes / Torquay / stop / the / train

31 I don't ...

Übersetzen Sie.

1. Ich mag dieses Zimmer nicht.
2. Wir wissen nicht, was passiert ist.
3. Er macht keinen Sport.
4. Zurzeit arbeite ich nicht.
5. Das ist doch nicht wirklich passiert?!
6. Ich habe nicht gewartet. Es war spät.
7. Wir wollten kein Taxi nehmen.
8. Er hat nicht viel Talent.

5. Fragen und Frageanhängsel

32. Who are you?
33. A or B?
34. How did you get there?
35. When do we arrive?
36. Questions, questions, questions
37. An interview
38. Which provider?
39. Talking to a lab technician
40. Right?
41. Right again?
42. That surprises me.

32 Who are you?

Was passt zusammen?

1. Who are
2. What sort of car
3. When does
4. Who
5. Who do
6. What did
7. Why have
8. What colours
9. Which colour

a. the match start?
b. knows the answer?
c. they invited that idiot?
d. are there?
e. has she got?
f. it cost?
g. is best, do you think?
h. you?
i. you know here?

1	2	3	4	5	6	7	8	9
h								

33 A or B?

Was ist richtig: a oder b?

1. When ... the problem start?
   a) did   b) has
2. Who ... the presentation?
   a) did give   b) gave
3. What ...? Maybe I can help.
   a) do you need   b) need you
4. Which hotel ... for you?
   a) they booked   b) did they book

1	2	3	4

34 How did you get there?

Ergänzen Sie die Frage.

1. ◆ How (get) _did you get_ here?
   ● I came by car.

2. ◆ (like) ______________________ Italian food?
   ● Oh yes! I love it!

3. ◆ (take) ______________________ anyone with you?
   ● Yes, I'm taking Fran and Megan.

4. ◆ (do) ______________________ anything interesting?
   ● Not really. We had a very lazy two days.

5. ◆ What (should / wear) ______________________?
   ● It doesn't really matter. They're always very informal.

6. ◆ Who (cook) ______________________ in your family when you were a kid?
   ● Actually it was mostly my dad.

7. ◆ Who (ask) ______________________ when you needed advice?
   ● That was usually my mum.

8. ◆ Who (go shopping) ______________________ in your family?
   ● I do!

35 When do we arrive?

Streichen Sie den falschen Satz durch.

1. Wann kommen wir an?
   a. ~~When we arrive?~~
   b. When do we arrive?

2. Was bedeutet dieses Wort?
   a. What does this word mean?
   b. What means this word?

3. Wen kennst du?
   a. Who know you?
   b. Who do you know?

4. Wie viel muss ich bezahlen?
   a. How much do I have to pay?
   b. How much do I must pay?

5. Brauchen Sie ein Taschentuch?
   a. Do you need a handkerchief?
   b. Need you a handkerchief?

6. Wer schreibt die Einladungen?
   a. Who is writing the invitations?
   b. Who does write the invitations?

36 Questions, questions, questions

Was passt zusammen?

1. Does Tina know about the meeting?
2. Will you be at Sandra's party?
3. Has the water boiled?
4. Did you get my message?
5. Can you see OK from where you're sitting?
6. Are you ready?
7. Did they reach an agreement?
8. Have the tickets come?

a. Yes, it has.
b. Yes, I did thanks.
c. Almost. Are you?
d. Not really. Can you?
e. No, I won't, I'm afraid.
f. No, I'm afraid they didn't.
g. Yes, they came in this morning's post.
h. Yes, she does.

1	2	3	4	5	6	7	8
h							

37 An interview

Ergänzen Sie.

- So where (1. you be) *were you* last night between 10.30 and midnight?
- At home, in bed.
- (2. anyone can) ______________________ confirm[1] that?
  (3. you be) ______________________ with anyone?
- That's none of your business!
- It may be in your interest to have a witness[2].
  When (4. you hear) ______________________ about the break-in at your office?
- This morning. My secretary called me.
- What time (5. you get) ______________________ this call?
- I don't know, 8.15, 8.30.
- (6. he know) ______________________ that the company is in serious financial difficulties?
- He's my secretary. I don't tell him everything.
- How long (7. you be) ______________________ in debt[3]?
- What does all this have to do with the break-in?
- That's what I am trying to find out.
  What (8. you do) ______________________ after you got the call?
- I called my insurance company[4].
- Why (9. you do) ______________________ that?
- Because that's what I didn't do the last time the offices were broken into! It was a big mistake.

[1] bestätigen
[2] Zeuge
[3] verschuldet
[4] Versicherungsgesellschaft

38 Which provider?

Ergänzen Sie die Frage.

1. Which provider (you / use) *do you use* ?
2. Which providers (be) __________ the most popular?
3. How many people (you / interview) __________ in last month's survey[1]?
4. How many people (come) __________ to last month's presentation?
5. What (interest) __________ people most at conferences like this?
6. What (people / like) __________ about conferences like this?
7. Who (phone) __________ the police? Was it you?
8. Who else (you / inform) __________? Did you tell Mr Roberts?
9. Where (you / be) __________? I've been looking for you everywhere.
10. Where (you / sit) __________? I didn't see you.

[1] Meinungsumfrage

39 Talking to a lab technician

Ergänzen Sie.

◆ Where (1. you come) *do you come* from?
● The north of England.
◆ And what (2. you do) ________________?
● I'm a lab technician[1].
◆ What sort of company (3. you work) ________________ for?
● A food manufacturer[2].
◆ (4. you be) ________________ with them a long time?
● Three years.
◆ (5. it be) _____________ an interesting job?
● It's OK.
◆ (6. you have to) _____________________ study or train a long time to get your qualifications?
● Quite a long time, but I didn't go to university.
◆ (7. you be) _____________ married? (8. you have) ________________ children?
● It's no on both of those.
◆ (9. you always live) ________________________ where you live now?
● No, I grew up near London.

[1] Laborant/in
[2] Lebensmittelhersteller

40 Right?

Was passt zusammen?

1. This is a lovely hotel,
2. A Danish company bought it,
3. You speak some French,
4. They haven't decided yet,
5. You can't swim,
6. Reg lives in Horsham,
7. The tyres need replacing,
8. It won't make a lot of difference,

a. don't you?
b. have they?
c. doesn't he?
d. don't they?
e. will it?
f. didn't they?
g. isn't it?
h. can you?

1	2	3	4	5	6	7	8
g							

41 Right again?

Ergänzen Sie das passende Frageanhängsel.

1. You don't like Phelps, *do you*?
2. We're going to be late, ______?
3. It didn't cost as much as last time, ______?
4. You'll be coming, ______?
5. John wasn't there, ______?
6. Gerda always looks so good, ______?
7. You eat meat, ______?

5

42 That surprises me.

Ergänzen Sie.

1. ◆ We're all quite worried.
   ● *Are you* ? I don't think there's any reason to be.

2. ◆ I can't believe that robots can do this job.
   ● *Can't you* ? They can do amazing things these days.

3. ◆ I don't want to go.
   ● ______________________? Whyever not? It's going to be a great event.

4. ◆ She loves anything exotic – oriental, African, Arabic.
   ● ______________________? I hope she eats 'normal' European food, too.

5. ◆ I know this film.
   ● ______________________? I've never seen it before.

6. ◆ They keep asking for more money.
   ● ______________________? Well, I would just refuse.

7. ◆ We ran out of petrol.
   ● ______________________? So how did you get here?

8. ◆ The snow didn't last.
   ● ______________________? So no skiing?

6. Zukunftsformen

43 I'll ...

Korrigieren Sie.

1. ~~Wait, I help you.~~
   Wait, I'll help you.
2. ~~I give you a hand.~~
   ____
3. ~~I lend you the money.~~
   ____
4. ~~I give you a lift.~~
   ____
5. Just a moment, ~~I get Simon for you.~~
   Just a moment, ______________________________
6. ~~He calls you back.~~
   ____
7. ~~I see if she's here.~~
   ____
8. ~~They let you know~~ as soon as possible.
   ______________________________ as soon as possible.

44 I'll have fish.

Ergänzen Sie.

◆ Are you ready to order?
● I think so. Amy? Have you decided?
■ (1. have) *I'll have* the fish, please.
◆ And what would you like with that? Salad or vegetables?
■ (2. take) ______ vegetables, please.
◆ And you, sir?
● I think (3. have) ______ the steak.
◆ Certainly, sir. And how would you like it?
● Medium, please. No, (4. have) ______ it rare.
◆ Certainly. And what would you like to drink?
● I think (5. we try) ______ the South African red. Is that OK with you, Amy?
■ Sure.
◆ It's a very nice wine, I can really recommend it. A bottle?
● Yes, please.
■ And (6. we take) ______ a bottle of mineral water, too.
◆ Sparkling or still?
■ Still, please.
◆ Any starters?
■ (7. not have) ______ anything, thanks.
● Nor me, thanks. (8. we have) ______ a dessert instead.

45 A or B?

Was stimmt: a oder b?

1. a) I expect we meet again in Frankfurt.
   b) I expect we'll meet again in Frankfurt.

2. a) He doesn't want to stay the night because he's leaving on a business trip the next morning.
   b) He will not stay the night because he's leaving on a business trip the next morning.

3. a) I have a feeling that something awful happens.
   b) I have a feeling that something awful is going to happen.

4. a) What do you do this Friday? Do you have time then?
   b) What are you doing this Friday? Do you have time then?

5. a) We don't go away this Christmas.
   b) We're not going away this Christmas.

6. a) We leave the dog with Karen's parents as usual.
   b) We'll be leaving the dog with Karen's parents as usual.

1	2	3	4	5	6
b					

46 All right?

Kreuzen Sie alle richtigen Lösungen an.

1. When we're in London next month,
   - a. we'll be staying with friends.
   - b. we're going to stay with friends.
   - c. we're staying with friends.
   - d. we stay with friends.

2. The weather forecast doesn't sound too good.
   - a. I expect it rains at the weekend.
   - b. I expect it'll rain at the weekend.
   - c. I expect it's going to rain at the weekend.
   - d. I expect it's raining at the weekend.

3. He's no longer a youngster!
   - a. He'll be 50 next year.
   - b. He'll be being 50 next year.
   - c. He's 50 next year.
   - d. He's going to be 50 next year.

4. How much wine should I get?
   - a. How many people are coming?
   - b. How many people are going to be coming?
   - c. How many people come?
   - d. How many people will be coming?

47 More than one option

Ergänzen Sie eine passende Zukunftsform.

1. The meeting tomorrow (only be) ______________________________ ________________ two hours.
2. Maybe there (not be) ______________________________ ______ enough time to discuss everything.
3. We (move) ______________________________ house next month.
4. This time next week I (lie) ______________________________ ______ on the beach.
5. By this time next week, we (do) ______________________________ _____________ most of the work.
6. When (you take) ______________________________ your exam?
7. I suppose (you have) ______________________________ ______ next Friday off.
8. Maybe the recession (not be) ______________________________ _________ as bad as all the experts are forecasting.
9. There's no point in rushing. The train (leave) _____________________ _____________________ by now.

7. Aktiv und Passiv

48 Record holders etc.

Ergänzen Sie.

a film • ~~a horror story~~ • a play • a series of children's books

J.K. Rowling • ~~Steven King~~ • Steven Spielberg • William Shakespeare

1. 

a horror story by Steven King

2. 

____

3. 

____

4. 

____

Und nun korrigieren Sie.

Michael Schumacher • Margaret Court

5. The record for tennis Grand Slam singles titles is held ~~from~~ ~~Serena Williams~~.
   It ________________.

6. The record for Formula 1 championships is held ~~from Juan Fangio~~.
   It ________________.

49 Who did it?

Was passt zusammen?

1. Someone has
2. Over 1000 hits
3. We are being
4. Over one million euros have
5. The road was
6. A far higher number of sales had
7. English is
8. Many of these places had not

a. asked to accept pay cuts.
b. been discovered as tourist destinations.
c. widened last year.
d. left a message on the answering machine.
e. been expected.
f. were recorded on the website within the first two minutes.
g. been spent.
h. spoken all over the world.

1	2	3	4	5	6	7	8
d							

50 A or B?

Was passt: a oder b?

1. We ... made to feel very unwelcome.
   a) was b) were

2. 'Yesterday' was a famous song ... the Beatles.
   a) by b) from

3. I couldn't get into the room because it ... .
   a) was being cleaned b) was cleaned

4. Where ...? I seem to recognize that tree.
   a) has this photo been taken b) was this photo taken?

5. Bags ... at reception.
   a) can be left b) can left

6. A new model ...
   a) has just been launched b) is just been launched

7. Reminders ... next week.
   a) will be sent out b) will send out

8. A lot of changes ... since then.
   a) are made b) have been made

9. ...
   a) By who was the brochure designed?
   b) Who was the brochure designed by?

10. We ... refreshing cold drinks when we arrived.
    a) were being offered b) were offered

1	2	3	4	5	6	7	8	9	10
b									

51 From active to passive

Wandeln Sie wie im Beispiel um.

1. Someone has made a serious mistake.
   A serious mistake has been made.
2. They'll tell us tomorrow.
   We ______________________ tomorrow.
3. They're still testing the system.
   The system ______________________
4. They didn't invite us.
   We ______________________
5. Someone was filming the event.
   The event ______________________
6. They are reprinting the book.
   The book ______________________
7. They ate up all the food in minutes!
   All the food ______________________ in minutes!
8. Nobody had expected such a huge crowd.
   Such a huge crowd ______________________
9. They are monitoring[1] all phone calls and emails.
   All phone calls and emails ______________________

[1] überwachen

52 Tourist questions

Übersetzen Sie.

1. Wann wurde das Schloss errichtet?
   When was the castle built?
2. Wann ist das Hotel eröffnet worden?
3. Wann werden die Koffer abgeholt [*collect*] (werden)?
4. Wo sind die Tickets ausgestellt [*issue*] worden?
5. Wie sind Sie informiert worden?
6. Wird der Briefkasten heute geleert [*empty*] (werden)?
7. Warum sind die Betten nicht gemacht worden?
8. Hat man unsere Bestellung vergessen?
9. Wird ein Trinkgeld erwartet?

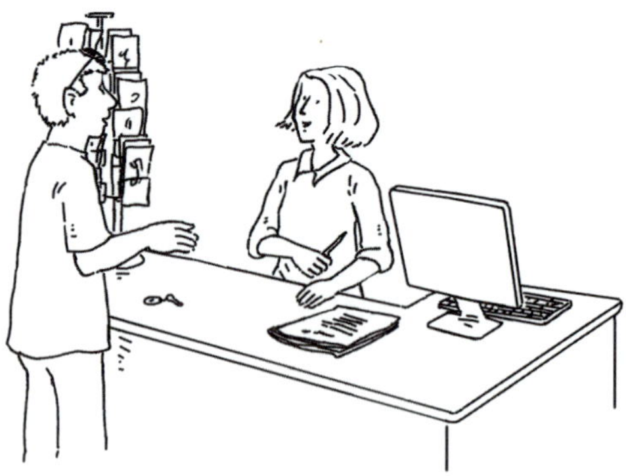

53 Who and/or what?

Was ist richtig: a, b oder a und b? Kreuzen Sie an.

1. We had to answer lots of questions.
   - a. We were asked lots of questions.
   - b. Lots of questions were asked.

2. Someone explained the rules to us.
   - a. The rules were explained to us.
   - b. We were explained the rules.

3. They offered me help with the removal costs[1] as part of the deal.
   - a. Help with the removal costs was offered as part of the deal.
   - b. I was offered help with the removal costs as part of the deal.

4. They gave us very little time to make up our mind.
   - a. Us was given very little time to make up our mind.
   - b. We were given very little time to make up our mind.

5. They promised me assistance.
   - a. Assistance was promised.
   - b. I was promised assistance.

6. They suggested that we should rethink the packaging.
   - a. It was suggested that we should rethink the packaging.
   - b. We were suggested to rethink the packaging.

7. They described the whole process in great detail.
   - a. The whole process was described in great detail.
   - b. We were described the whole process in great detail.

[1] Umzugskosten

54 Who did it?

Ergänzen Sie die Rückfragen, indem Sie das Passiv verwenden.

1. A famous British architect designed the museum.
   Sorry. Who was it designed by ?
2. They've deposited the key with the neighbours.
   Sorry, who ______________________ with?
3. The interim manager will inform the workforce.
   Sorry. Who ______________________ ?
4. Local business people are sponsoring the event.
   Sorry, who ______________________ ?
5. The CEO signed the letter.
   Sorry, who ______________________ ?
6. The company has been taken over by a foreign investor.
   Sorry, who ______________________ ?
7. Edison invented it.
   Sorry, who ______________________ ?
8. The government is going to bail the company out[1].
   Sorry, who ______________________ ?

[1] eine Bürgschaft übernehmen für

8. Infinitiv und Gerundium

55 A or B?

Was passt: a oder b?

1. a) I hope to be able to come.
   b) I hope being able to come.

2. a) We've just finished repairing the broken window.
   b) We've just finished to repair the broken window.

3. a) I suggested calling Alexander and asking him.
   b) I suggested to call Alexander and ask him.

4. a) I'd like trying to learn Dutch.
   b) I'd like to try and learn Dutch.

5. a) We've decided to wait.
   b) We've decided waiting.

6. a) I've given up to try.
   b) I've given up trying.

7. a) You can't avoid making mistakes on a project like this.
   b) You can't avoid to make mistakes on a project like this.

8. a) I refuse taking no as an answer.
   b) I refuse to take no as an answer.

9. a) I don't mind paying a bit extra if the quality is good.
   b) I don't mind to pay a bit extra if the quality is good.

10. a) I can't imagine doing your job.
    b) I can't imagine to do your job.

11. a) We're looking forward to see you again.
    b) We're looking forward to seeing you again.

1	2	3	4	5	6	7	8	9	10	11
a										

56 Do you enjoy cooking?

Ergänzen Sie die richtige Form.

1. ◆ Do you enjoy (cook) *cooking* for a big crowd?
   ● Yes, I do. And I like (try out) ________________ new recipes.

2. ◆ Don't do it! You'll risk (make) ________________ an enemy of the man. And that's something you'd regret (do) ________________ till the end of your days.
   ● What would you recommend (do) ________________ then?

3. ◆ We need to practise (do) ________________ this in a hurry.
   ● Yes, we don't want (make) ________________ any mistakes.

4. ◆ Can you remind me (ask) ________________ Jill for the address?
   ● I can't promise (remember) ________________.

5. ◆ It's no use (worry) ________________.
   ● No, you're right. There's no point (get) ________________ anxious.
   ◆ Just stop (worry) ________________ and hope for the best.

6. ◆ I was looking forward to (enjoy) ________________ a nice long lazy weekend. I felt like (stay) ________________ in bed all weekend. But then Martin decided (do) ________________ a lot of work in the garden.

57 He seems to like behaving badly.

Sortieren Sie die Teile und bilden Sie Sätze. Achtung: Je ein Teil wird nicht benötigt!

1. badly / behaving / he / liking / seems / to like
   He seems to like behaving badly.
2. a lift / I / giving / offered / them / to give
   ______
3. at the café / don't / me / meeting / mention / to meet
   ______
4. admit / being / I / there / to be
   ______
5. asking for / help / I / really dislike / to ask
   ______
6. can't / carry on / like this / meeting / to meet / we
   ______
7. closing / discussed / the factory in Poland / they / to close
   ______
8. about it / claims / having / he / known / nothing / to have
   ______

58 Would you like ...?

Korrigieren Sie.

1. ~~Would you like that I help you?~~
   Would you like me to help you?

2. ~~Would you like that we wait for you?~~
   ______________________________ for you?

3. ~~I'd like that you go to the conference for us.~~
   ______________________________ to the conference for us.

4. ~~I want that you completely redo this.~~
   ______________________________ completely redo this.

5. ~~Does he really expect that I work every weekend?~~
   ______________________________ every weekend?

6. ~~I need that you pick up the children from school.~~
   ______________________________ the children from school.

7. ~~Would you like that I shut the window?~~
   ______________________________ the window?

8. ~~Do you want that I take Sven to the airport?~~
   ______________________________ Sven to the airport?

9. ~~I'd love that he makes just one mistake.~~
   ______________________________ just one mistake.

59 I saw it happen.

Unterstreichen Sie die richtige Form.

1. I saw it (a.) happen / (b.) to happen.
2. We've decided not (a.) book / (b.) to book in advance.
3. Just don't let this (a.) happen / (b.) to happen again!
4. Can you get someone (a.) clear up / (b.) to clear up the room?
5. We should (a.) leave / (b.) to leave fairly soon because of the traffic.
6. I'll make them (a.) pay / (b.) to pay for this!
7. They won't let me (a.) park / (b.) to park any closer.
8. Did you hear the police cars (a.) pass by / (b.) to pass by?

1	2	3	4	5	6	7	8
a							

60 She accused me.

Was passt zusammen?

1. She accused me
2. Banks were criticized
3. The protesters were prevented
4. They thanked us
5. I'm very proud
6. There's no real alternative
7. Is there any chance
8. We've had little success

a. from entering the building by the police.
b. of doing it all by myself.
c. to flying. It's too far away.
d. of finding a flat for under 600 euros?
e. of trying to manoeuvre her out of her job.
f. for looking after their cat.
g. in finding a replacement for Sarah Johnson.
h. for lending to people who weren't creditworthy.

1	2	3	4	5	6	7	8
e							

61 *By, instead, without, …*

Wandeln Sie wie im Beispiel um.

1. If you book online, you can save quite a bit. (by)
   You can save quite a bit by booking online.
2. Let's not go on the bus, but let's take a taxi. (instead)
   ______________ instead of ______________
3. I asked the question. I didn't even think. (without)
   ______________ without ______________
4. If you read a lot, you can improve your vocabulary. (by)
   ______________ by ______________
5. Scan the mail attachment for viruses, then open it. (before)
   Before ______________
6. We drove all the way. We didn't stop. (without)
   ______________ without ______________
7. I won't have coffee, I'll take tea for a change. (instead)
   Instead ______________
8. He invested in the stock market and lost a lot of money. (by)
   ______________ by ______________

62 What are you afraid of?

Ergänzen Sie. Die Präpositionen können mehrmals eingesetzt werden.

at • for • in • of • on

1. I'm always afraid _of_ making a mistake.
2. I'd be interested ______ finding out more.
3. Sandra's good ______ dealing with this sort of problem.
4. I got tired ______ waiting and left.
5. Are you in favour ______ commissioning[1] a new translation?
6. I don't believe ______ being soft on[2] beginners.
7. Do you have any specific reason ______ asking this?
8. I'm grateful to you ______ informing me so promptly.
9. I'd like to congratulate you ______ making such a good choice.
10. Is there any point ______ continuing with this?

[1] in Auftrag geben
[2] nachsichtig sein gegenüber

63 A or B?

Was stimmt: a oder b?

1. a) I must remember calling Janine and ask her how she got on at her interview.
   b) I must remember to call Janine and ask her how she got on at her interview.

2. a) Have you forgotten losing our way when we went there the first time?
   b) Have you forgotten to lose our way when we went there the first time?

3. a) I forgot paying the bill, and now they've sent a reminder.
   b) I forgot to pay the bill, and now they've sent a reminder.

4. a) Don't you remember meeting them in Amsterdam once, quite by chance?
   b) Don't you remember to meet them in Amsterdam once, quite by chance?

5. a) I stopped on the way down once to stretch my legs.
   b) I stopped on the way down once stretching my legs.

6. a) I've stopped even opening all these junk-mail newsletters.
   b) I've stopped even to open all these junk-mail newsletters.

7. a) I meant to ask you: have you got your money back yet?
   b) I meant asking you: have you got your money back yet?

8. a) Flying with a budget airline usually means getting up in the middle of the night.
   b) Flying with a budget airline usually means to get up in the middle of the night.

1	2	3	4	5	6	7	8
b							

9. *if*-Sätze

64 *If* or *when*?

Ergänzen Sie.

1. I'm meeting Ann next week. _When_ I see her, I'll tell her what you need.
2. Would it be OK ________ I came a little later?
3. I'll do the plan ________ I have all the data. That should be by tomorrow at the latest.
4. ________ Jonathan agrees, we can borrow his boat.
5. ________ the weather stays fine, we could have a barbecue.
6. ________ it's fine, we often have a barbecue.
7. I don't know what I would do ________ I didn't have you to help me.
8. ________ you get stuck, give me a call.
9. ________ I'm not there, just take a taxi.

65 With or without *will*?

Unterstreichen Sie die richtige Form.

1. When I sleep in old buildings, I (a.) seem / (b.) will seem to dream more.
2. (a.) We eat / (b.) We'll eat when Jack gets here. He said he'd be here by seven.
3. When I see Mervin, (a.) I check / (b.) I'll check if he's got everything he needs.
4. If they find out, (a.) there's / (b.) there will be problems.

66 If I know ...

Was passt zusammen?

1. If I know the answer by this evening,
2. What would you have done
3. What will you do
4. They'll be here by six
5. They'd be here by six
6. They would have been here by six
7. What would you do
8. If I knew the answer,
9. If I had known the answer then,

a. if your firm moved its base to another country?
b. if there are no problems with the traffic.
c. if they left at four.
d. if I hadn't warned you?
e. if they hadn't had that breakdown.
f. I'll let you know.
g. if the weather's bad?
h. I wouldn't have to ask you!
i. we would have been saved a lot of trouble.

1	2	3	4	5	6	7	8	9
f								

67 What's wrong?

Korrigieren Sie die *if*-Sätze.

1. ~~It would be better if I would have more time.~~
   It would be better if I had more time.

2. ~~If you will want, I can come back later.~~
   ______________________, __________ come back later.

3. ~~If I would have seen you, I had stopped.~~
   ____

4. ~~It made me feel happier if I would be more prepared.~~
   ______________ feel happier, ______________ more prepared.

5. ~~If it wouldn't been cheaper, I didn't buy it from a foreign company.~~
   ____
   from a foreign company.

6. ~~Where would you live if you can choose?~~
   ____

7. ~~They hadn't invited me to the meeting if Hannah didn't said something.~~
   ____________________________ to the meeting __________
   ______________ something.

8. ~~We fly on a weekday if we would have the choice.~~
   ______________ on a weekday ________________ the choice.

68 I'll deal with it.

Ergänzen Sie die richtige Form.

1. I (deal) *will deal* with it this weekend if I have time.
2. She says she (be) ________________ back at work on Monday if all goes well.
3. If he had recognized the warning signs, he (not be) ________________ ________________ so surprised at what happened.
4. If you (not drink) ________________ wine in the evenings, you would sleep much better.
5. If Ronald (call) ________________, can you ask him to leave a message, please?
6. What (you / do) ________________________ if they had said there were no places left?
7. If I (have) ________________ their mobile number, I could give them a call.
8. If we (can) ________________ sell our house for a decent price, we might move.
9. Think how much better things would be if everyone (have) ________________ their own room.
10. If I (not see) ________________ it with my own eyes, I (not believe) ________________________ it!
11. If Noel (not go) ________________ to that exhibition, he (never meet) ________________________ Sophie.
12. If I (not read) ________________ the book, I (not understand) ________________________ the movie.

69 If ..., then ...

Übersetzen Sie.

1. Wenn der Bus nicht bald kommt, gehe ich zu Fuß.

2. Ich hätte nicht ja gesagt, wenn ich Zweifel gehabt *[be in doubt]* hätte.

3. Ich würde dir helfen, wenn ich wüsste wie.

4. Wenn er mich noch einmal Fritzi nennt, bringe ich ihn um!

5. Wenn wir verloren hätten, wäre es nicht das Ende der Welt gewesen.

6. Es wäre schrecklich, wenn wir das Wetter kontrollieren könnten.

7. Auch wenn sie es mir schenken würden, würde ich es nicht haben wollen.

8. Wenn ich die richtige Kleidung mitgenommen hätte, hätte ich nicht die ganze Woche gefroren.

9. Wenn die Firma nicht diese riskanten Investitionen getätigt hätte, wäre sie nicht bankrott gegangen *[go bankrupt]*.

10. Modalverben

70 Does Bernd have to ...?

Was passt zusammen?

1. Does
2. Am
3. Do
4. Are
5. He wasn't
6. It could
7. He must
8. There might not
9. You might have

a. you able to take a day off?
b. be crazy to do that.
c. allowed to ask questions.
d. told me!
e. I allowed to take photos?
f. be time.
g. Bernd have to go to school on Saturdays?
h. happen any time.
i. you have to ask permission?

1	2	3	4	5	6	7	8	9
g								

71 I can't swim.

Ergänzen Sie.

~~can't~~ • couldn't • might not • mustn't • shall • will • would

1. I'm very embarrassed[1] about the fact that I _can't_ swim.
2. ______________ I see if he's there?
3. We ______________ be able to come. I'll let you know tomorrow.
4. You ______________ do that! There'll be big problems if they find out.
5. Anna ______________ come because she was away on business.
6. ______________ you agree that this is not the best time to try and sell?
7. I just heard the door. That ______________ be Andy.

[1] verlegen

72 *Mustn't or needn't?*

Ergänzen Sie.

1. You ______________ laugh. It's a serious matter.
2. You ______________ hurry. We've still got lots of time.
3. I ______________ forget to take a camera.
4. The Thompsons ______________ worry. Nobody is going to build a supermarket in a neighbourhood like this.
5. Frank and Joel ______________ attend. I know they have more important things to do.
6. Something like that ______________ cost a lot of money.

73 Can do!

Ergänzen Sie das fehlende Wort.

1. Ich kann Französisch.
   I can __________ French.
2. Bitte schreib du die Karte. Du kannst es so gut.
   You write the card please. You can __________ it so well.

74 I've been able to contact him.

Ergänzen Sie die richtige Form.

could have • ~~couldn't~~ • haven't been able to • wasn't able to • weren't able to • won't be able to

1. I've managed to speak to Jack at last. I _couldn't_ get hold of him yesterday.
2. From next week you ______________ park here any more. They're going to start building on the site.
3. I'm still looking for a present. I ______________ find anything suitable yet.
4. We would have loved to stay longer, but we ______________. We had to get back.
5. Sven wasn't at the meeting, so I ______________ ask him.
6. The effects ______________ been much worse. We were very lucky.

had to • ~~will have to~~ • will have to • won't have to

7. It's no good. We _will have to_ ask for more time.
8. I ______________ wait over two hours. I was really angry!
9. You ______________ be more careful in future.
10. Don't worry. You ______________ say anything.

75 *Have to*

Korrigieren Sie.

1. I ~~hadn't to~~ wait very long.
   I *didn't have to* wait very long.
2. What ~~have we to~~ do?
   What ______________________ do?
3. When ~~have we to~~ be there?
   When ______________________ be there?
4. Why ~~must you~~ say that? That was stupid.
   Why ______________________ say that? That was stupid.
5. The work ~~mustn't~~ be handed in till Monday.
   The work ______________________ be handed in till Monday.
6. I was really quite surprised. We ~~mustn't~~ show any ID.
   I was really quite surprised. We ______________________ show any ID.
7. How long ~~had you to~~ wait?
   How long ______________________ wait?
8. If your flight's at 6.30 tomorrow morning, ~~mustn't you~~ get up very early?
   If your flight's at 6.30 tomorrow morning, ______________________ get up very early?

76 All right?

Kreuzen Sie alle richtigen Lösungen an.

1. I'm afraid I can't let you in just like that.
   - a. Can I see your ID, please?
   - b. Could I see your ID, please?
   - c. May I see your ID, please?

2. I'm afraid I have to ask you to leave.
   - a. It isn't allowed to use mobile phones here.
   - b. You can't to use mobile phones here.
   - c. You aren't allowed to use mobile phones here.

3. They seem to have changed things.
   - a. We've never been allowed to park here before.
   - b. We've never can park here before.
   - c. We've never could park here before.

4. Where's Jack? He organized this meeting.
   - a. He can't have forgotten, can he?
   - b. He can't have forgotten, has he?
   - c. He mustn't have forgotten, must he?

5. I don't think we can just march in and help ourselves.
   - a. We had better to ask first.
   - b. We ought to ask first.
   - c. We should ask first.

77 *Have to, may, etc.*

Ergänzen Sie in der richtigen Zeitform.

1. Es kann sein, dass sie unsere Pässe sehen wollen.
   They ____________ want to see our passports.

2. Es könnte sein, dass ich nicht komme.
   I ____________ not come.

3. Es kann morgen regnen. Wir wissen es nicht.
   It ____________ rain tomorrow. We don't know.

4. Konnten sie den Fehler finden?
   ________________________ find the fault?

5. Musstet ihr etwas unterschreiben?
   ________________________ sign anything?

6. Auf diesen Augenblick habe ich lange warten müssen.
   I ____________________ wait a long time for this moment.

7. Es darf nicht passieren.
   It ____________________ happen.

8. Ich weiß nicht, mit wem sie spricht. Es kann Peter sein.
   I don't know who she's talking to. It _______________ be Peter.

78 A or B?

Was stimmt: a oder b?

1. a) When you lost your job, it must be very difficult for you.
   b) When you lost your job, it must have been very difficult for you.

2. a) I may can help you. Ask me again tomorrow.
   b) I may be able to help you. Ask me again tomorrow.

3. a) Fantastic. You must be feeling over the moon[1]!
   b) Fantastic. You must feeling over the moon!

4. a) Things could been worse, so I shouldn't complain.
   b) Things could have been worse, so I shouldn't complain.

5. a) To have to sit and watch and not be able to do anything was the hardest part.
   b) To must to sit and watch and not be able to do anything was the hardest part.

1	2	3	4	5
b				

[1] überglücklich

11. Artikel und Begleiter

79 On Monday

Was passt zusammen?

1. You can tell me when I see you on
2. We meet on the
3. The next meeting is on
4. We meet for
5. We don't meet so often in the
6. There's a break in

a. the second of March.
b. summer.
c. brunch.
d. August.
e. first Saturday in the month.
f. Friday.

1	2	3	4	5	6
f					

80 Twice a month

Korrigieren Sie.

1. We meet ~~twice in the month~~.
   We meet *twice a month*.
2. Fresh rolls are baked ~~four times in the day~~.
   Fresh rolls are baked ______.
3. There's a bus to the local town only ~~twice in the week~~.
   There's a bus to the local town only ______.
4. It's the sort of thing that happens ~~once in the lifetime~~.
   It's the sort of thing that happens ______.

81 A or B?

Was stimmt: a oder b?

1. a) Our son is training as a teacher.
   b) Our son is training as teacher.

2. a) My boss is a workaholic.
   b) My boss is workaholic.

3. a) Why are you always in a such hurry?
   b) Why are you always in such a hurry?

4. a) What a beautiful day!
   b) What for a beautiful day!

5. a) What a beautiful weather!
   b) What beautiful weather!

6. a) Tony is a golfer.
   b) Tony is golfer.

7. a) He's a member of several clubs.
   b) He's member of several clubs.

8. a) Please have a seat.
   b) Please take seat.

1	2	3	4	5	6	7	8
a							

82 They argued and argued.

Was passt zusammen?

1. They argued all weekend, almost without
2. We need to look at the system as
3. What do you do for
4. I haven't seen Amy for
5. Let's just stay at home for
6. Oh dear, what

a. a living?
b. a long time.
c. a whole.
d. a break.
e. a pity.
f. a change.

1	2	3	4	5	6
d					

83 I'm a teacher.

Übersetzen Sie.

1. Ich bin Lehrerin.
   I'm a teacher.
2. Es war so eine furchtbare Reise.
3. Was für ein Auto fährt er?
4. Was für ein herrliches Wetter!
5. Wir treffen uns einmal im Monat.

84 A or B?

Was stimmt: a oder b?

1. a) Where do your children go to school?
   b) Where do your children go to the school?

2. a) They are closing school in Green Street.
   b) They are closing the school in Green Street.

3. a) When was church built?
   b) When was the church built?

4. a) Do people in this country still go to church?
   b) Do people in this country still go to the church?

5. a) At least half the people didn't notice anything.
   b) At least the half of the people didn't notice anything.

6. a) Most people were asleep.
   b) The most people were asleep.

7. a) Who got most the votes[1]?
   b) Who got the most votes?

8. a) It's been like this all week.
   b) It's been like this the all week.

1	2	3	4	5	6	7	8
a							

[1] Stimmen

85 St. Pancras Station

Ergänzen Sie *the*, wenn es nötig ist.

1. Eurostar trains arrive at _–_ St. Pancras Station.
2. Which river runs through London? Is it ______ Thames?
3. I love ______ Alps.
4. I have no plan to climb ______ Mount Everest.
5. She lives in ______ Half Moon Street.
6. The biggest lake in Africa is ______ Lake Victoria.
7. We land at ______ Gatwick Airport, not Heathrow.
8. My favourite London park is ______ Green Park.
9. Everybody knows ______ Tower Bridge.
10. Where exactly are ______ Ardennes?

86 A friend

Übersetzen Sie.

1. Tim ist ein Freund von mir.

   ____

2. Andrea ist eine Kollegin von Julia.

   ____

3. Ein Bruder von Jack fährt einen alten Jaguar.

   ____

4. Nachbarn von uns haben ein Haus in Spanien.

   ____

87 Love

Ergänzen Sie die Übersetzung.

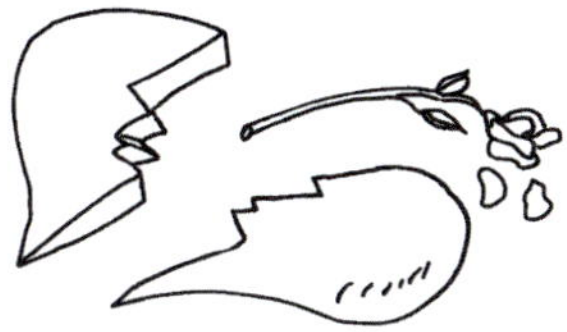

1. Die Liebe hält nie, oder?
   Love never lasts, does it?
2. Welches Land ist der Geburtsort der Demokratie?
   Which country is the birthplace of ____________________?
3. Die Geschichte unserer Stadt begann vor 800 Jahren.
   ____________________ of our town began 800 years ago.
4. Es hat mehrere große Präsidenten in der amerikanischen Geschichte gegeben.
   There have been several great presidents in ____________________.
5. Das Leben und der Tod gehören zusammen.
   ____________________ and ____________________ belong together.
6. Wann hast du von dem Tod erfahren?
   When did you hear about ____________________?
7. Das Leben ist ein Abenteuer.
   ____________________ is an adventure.
8. Wie die Zeit vergeht!
   How ____________________ flies!
9. Welche Partei ist nicht für die Freiheit?
   Which party does not stand for ____________________?
10. Schau: die Schönheiten der Natur!
    Look: the beauties of ____________________!

88 All right?

Kreuzen Sie alle richtigen Lösungen an.

1.
- a. I know nearly all people in this room.
- b. I know nearly all the people in this room.
- c. I know the people in this room nearly all.

2.
- a. I know all in our street.
- b. I know every in our street.
- c. I know everyone in our street.

3.
- a. Both skiers were injured.
- b. Both the skiers were injured.
- c. The both skiers were injured.

4.
- a. Neither hotel has any rooms left.
- b. Neither of the two hotels has any rooms left.
- c. The hotels have neither any rooms left.

5.
- a. Nobody of us knew about it.
- b. None of us knew about it.
- c. No one of us knew about it.

12. Singular und Plural

89 Boxes

Wandeln Sie wie im Beispiel um.

1. What's this box doing here?
   What are these *boxes* doing here?

2. A new business has been opened.
   Several new ________________ have been opened.

3. Do you have the address?
   Do you have the ________________?

4. Can you make a copy, please?
   Can you make some ________________, please?

5. I don't want a green tomato, I want a ripe one!
   I don't want green ________________, I want ripe ________________!

6. Jason is my brother-in-law. My other brother-in-law is called Alan.
   Jason and Alan are my ________________________.

7. There's an interesting new series on TV.
   There are several interesting new ________________ on TV.

8. I'd love to see a wolf in the wild.
   I'd love to see ________________ in the wild.

9. We have a fox, a mouse and a sheep.
   We have ________________, ________________ and ________________.

10. I have a tooth that's causing problems.
    I have two ________________ that are causing problems.

90 A or B?

Was stimmt: a oder b?

1. a) We've just received an interesting new information.
   b) We've just received some interesting new information.

2. a) Let me give you an advice.
   b) Let me give you a piece of advice.

3. a) Her hair was a different colour when I saw her last.
   b) Her hairs were a different colour when I saw her last.

4. a) This furniture is old, but comfortable.
   b) These furniture are old, but comfortable.

5. a) The damage was enormous.
   b) The damages were enormous.

6. a) These spaghetti are cold!
   b) This spaghetti is cold!

7. a) It was a difficult task.
   b) It was a difficult work.

8. a) She speaks a very good English.
   b) She speaks very good English.

9. a) Progress is slow.
   b) Progress are slow.

10. a) This room is absolute chaos!
    b) This room is an absolute chaos!

1	2	3	4	5	6	7	8	9	10
b									

91 Where are my glasses?

Übersetzen Sie.

1. Wo ist meine Brille?
   Where _are my glasses_ ?
2. Wo ist die Polizei?
   Where ______________________________?
3. Ich habe drei Hosen gepackt.
   I've packed three ______________________.
4. Die USA haben große Probleme.
   The USA ______________ great problems.
5. In Zeiten wie diesen sind drei Prozent Zinsen viel.
   In times like these three per cent interest ____________ a lot.
6. Die Schere ist auf dem Tisch.
   ____________________ on the table.
7. Die Ware kommt morgen.
   ____________________ coming tomorrow.
8. Die Nachrichten sind gut.
   ____________________ good.
9. Die Treppe ist steil.
   ____________________ steep.

13. Adjektiv und Adverb

92. A or B?

93. *Bad* and *badly*

94. Odd one out

95. *Careful* or *carefully*?

96. Right or wrong?

97. Trends

98. A or B?

99. Here or there?

100. Every day

13

92 A or B?

Was passt: a oder b?

1. Have you spoken to Jenny ...?
   a) late　　b) lately
2. We arrived back very ... yesterday evening.
   a) late　　b) lately
3. I feel ... tired.
   a) incredible　　b) incredibly
4. Have you ever seen such an ... performance?
   a) incredible　　b) incredibly
5. How ... do you know them?
   a) good　　b) well
6. I hadn't been feeling very ... so I went to the doctor's.
   a) good　　b) well
7. I was never very ... at maths.
   a) good　　b) well
8. This sort of weather is ..., even for this part of the world.
   a) extreme　　b) extremely
9. The service is ... unreliable[1].
   a) extreme　　b) extremely
10. It was ... to see some new faces at last.
    a) wonderful refreshingly　　b) wonderfully refreshing

1	2	3	4	5	6	7	8	9	10
b									

[1] unzuverlässig

93 *Bad and badly*

Was passt zusammen?

1. I slept
2. I had a really
3. I've never stayed in such a
4. The man in the next room snored
5. At four o'clock there was a
6. I don't know what it was. I
7. I felt pretty
8. I complained

a. noisy hotel room.
b. sudden loud noise.
c. badly last night.
d. suddenly heard it.
e. noisily all night long.
f. angrily to the management.
g. bad night.
h. angry.

1	2	3	4	5	6	7	8
c							

94 Odd one out

Streichen Sie, was nicht passt.

1. quickly – ~~friendly~~ – especially – happily
2. slowly – carefully – well – madly
3. fast – early – hard – happy
4. automatically – basically – ethnically – publicly

95 *Careful or carefully?*

Ergänzen Sie die richtige Form.

careful

1. Listen _*carefully*_ to what I have to say.
2. Be ________________ what you do with that knife.

excited

3. You look ________________. Is something about to happen?
4. We heard a car pull up outside, and Janine looked ________________ out of the window.

particular

5. Was there any ________________ colour you were looking for?
6. The sofa was a ________________ horrid[1] colour.

lovely

7. This tastes ________________.
8. It's a ________________ meal.

anxious

9. ________________ glances passed between them, but neither of them said anything.
10. You seem ________________. What's the matter?

[1] fürchterlich

96 Right or wrong?

Korrigieren Sie den *kursiv* gedruckten Teil, falls nötig.

1. Three people arrived *early*, nobody arrived late.
   korrekt
2. You are very *good informed*.
3. In this sort of job you really have to work *hardly*.
4. His first wife died *tragicly* in a car accident.
5. The country has a *goodly* developed economy.
6. It was *hardly* necessary to point out Ferrow's mistake yet again.
7. The children are all very *good behaved*.
8. He's a very *good-natured* dog and would never bite anyone.

97 Trends

Korrigieren Sie.

1. Sales are much ~~badder~~ ________________ than in the same period last year.
2. They are 20% ~~more low~~ ________________.
3. It's not getting ~~easyer~~ ________________ to make forecasts[1].
4. Things were much ~~more better~~ ________________ ten years ago.
5. We've sold the ~~lest~~ ________________ number of units in our luxury range.
6. They are of course much ~~expensiver as~~ ______________________________ mass-market models.
7. The crisis has come much ~~sooner as~~ ____________________ expected.
8. Many of my colleagues are much ~~more surprised as I~~ ________________ ______________________.
9. They don't have the same kind of overview ~~like I~~ ____________________.
10. This is not the ~~most easyest~~ ____________________ business to be in in a time of crisis.

[1] Prognosen

98 A or B?

Was passt: a oder b?

1. a) You must always be prepared!
   b) You must be prepared always!

2. a) I usually am ready first.
   b) I am usually ready first.

3. a) We don't often watch TV.
   b) We don't watch often TV.

4. a) She drinks never alcohol.
   b) She never drinks alcohol.

5. a) I had an accident yesterday.
   b) I had yesterday an accident.

6. a) I'm still waiting for a reply.
   b) I'm waiting still for a reply.

7. a) They've announced just some job losses.
   b) They've just announced some job losses.

8. a) I do every day the same. It's so boring.
   b) I do the same every day. It's so boring.

9. a) She's flying next week to Trinidad.
   b) She's flying to Trinidad next week.

10. a) There probably won't be enough time.
    b) There won't probably be enough time.

1	2	3	4	5	6	7	8	9	10
a									

99 Here or there?

Markieren Sie die richtige Stellung des Adverbs.

1. (easily) We can (a.) X reach (b.) ____ Chicago by nightfall.
2. (slowly) The rain (a.) ____ is (b.) ____ starting to clear.
3. (usually) The process (a.) ____ doesn't take (b.) ____ this long.
4. (certainly) I (a.) ____ don't (b.) ____ agree.
5. (quickly) He (a.) ____ found (b.) ____ a new job.
6. (eventually) I (a.) ____ got (b.) ____ to sleep.
7. (soon) You'll (a.) ____ forget (b.) ____ the whole thing.
8. (soon) You'll (a.) ____ have forgotten (b.) ____ the whole thing.

100 Every day

Übersetzen Sie.

1. Ich nehme jeden Tag meine Medizin.
____
2. Ich sehe dich wahrscheinlich bald wieder.
____
3. So ein altes Auto kaufe ich nie wieder!
____
4. Sie verließ vor zehn Minuten das Büro.
____

14. Präpositionen

14

101 A or B?

Was stimmt: a oder b?

1. a) Brighton is at the coast.
   b) Brighton is on the coast.

2. a) There wasn't a cloud at the sky.
   b) There wasn't a cloud in the sky.

3. a) Everest is the highest mountain in the world.
   b) Everest is the highest mountain of the world.

4. a) Is the Dead Sea below sea level?
   b) Is the Dead Sea under sea level?

5. a) Who were you at the phone with for so long?
   b) Who were you on the phone to for so long?

6. a) Come and sit beside me.
   b) Come and sit besides me.

7. a) What are you doing at Christmas?
   b) What are you doing on Christmas?

8. a) We'll be by Janet's parents at Christmas Day.
   b) We'll be with Janet's parents on Christmas Day.

1	2	3	4	5	6	7	8

102 *At, in* or *on?*

Ergänzen Sie.

1. I suggest we meet *at* the entrance.
2. The party is ______ Jane's house.
3. I'll be ______ the office all day.
4. The company's offices are ______ 17 Spring Gardens.
5. ______ the weekend I like to get out of town.
6. They have a cottage ______ the country.
7. There's somebody ______ the door.
8. There were some expensive-looking prints ______ the wall.
9. I've spent the whole day ______ my computer.
10. I'll be ______ a conference in Bilbao next week.
11. How much time do you spend _____ the internet?
12. Who's the person ______ this photo?
13. Mason is ______ the doctor's. He's not feeling well.
14. I had to stop ______ the traffic lights.
15. Actually I hate lying ______ the beach.

103 Not before lunch

Ergänzen Sie.

1. I'll meet you ______ lunch, not before.
2. We'll see you ______ Monday.
3. When there is a full moon, it's not really dark ______ night.
4. I sometimes sit next to her ______ lunch.
5. What are you doing ______ 1st May?
6. Isn't your birthday ______ June?
7. I haven't spoken to him ______ last week.
8. It happened while I was ______ work.
9. What's ______ TV tonight?
10. Have you always lived ______ this address?
11. I would love to live ______ the sea.
12. My office is ______ the third floor.
13. I have no time ______ the moment, I'm afraid.
14. I moved here ______ the age of 12.
15. I've lived here now ______ over 20 years.

104 A or B?

Was stimmt: a oder b?

1. a) We should get to the airport by ten past seven.
   b) We should get to the airport till ten past seven.

2. a) I waited by seven o'clock, but he didn't call back.
   b) I waited till seven o'clock, but he didn't call back.

3. a) I have to finish this by Monday evening.
   b) I have to finish this till Monday evening.

105 Right or wrong?

Korrigieren Sie den *kursiv* gedruckten Teil, falls nötig.

1. The opening ceremony is *at 10.30 in the morning.*
   korrekt
2. He usually has the children *on the last Saturday in the month.*
   ______
3. I'm sure the topic will come up sometime *while the meeting.*
   ______
4. It all happened *for several years.*
   ______
5. It should arrive *till Tuesday* at the latest.
   ______
6. I'll be here *up to at least eight.*
   ______
7. We should know *within the next week.*
   ______
8. We live *nearby Oxford.*
   ______

106 A or B?

Was stimmt: a oder b?

1. Von wem ist das Buch? Kenne ich den Autor?
   a) Who is the book by?
   b) Who is the book from?

2. Wir sind alle gegen den Vorschlag.
   a) We are all against the suggestion.
   b) We are all contra the suggestion.

3. Wie viel Wein sollten wir pro Person einplanen?
   a) How much wine should we plan per person?
   b) How much wine should we plan pro person?

4. Es wurde wegen des Wetters verschoben.
   a) It was postponed because the weather.
   b) It was postponed because of the weather.

5. Es kommt auf die Chefin an. Sie entscheidet.
   a) It's on the boss. She decides.
   b) It's up to the boss. She decides.

6. Wir erwarten bis zu 500 Personen.
   a) We're expecting until 500 people.
   b) We're expecting up to 500 people.

7. Es kann nicht bis morgen warten.
   a) It can't wait by tomorrow.
   b) It can't wait till tomorrow.

8. Sie bauen sowohl Fabriken als auch Hotels.
   a) They build factories as well as hotels.
   b) They build factories as well than hotels.

107 In my opinion

Ergänzen Sie.

about • above • at • besides • except • ~~in~~ • of • on (2x) • to

1. _In_ my opinion this is all going to cost too much.
2. Everyone was there ______ Tina, who was on holiday.
3. We are ahead ______ schedule, which is absolutely fantastic!
4. How much do visitors spend ______ average?
5. If I don't get there ______ time, start without me.
6. According ______ Mr Watkins this is "absolutely normal".
7. I'm calling ______ the email you sent.
8. I'm having to do Pia's job ______ my own.
9. It's ______ all the cost that is worrying me.
10. There were ______ least 80 applicants for the job.

108 I'm tired of it.

Ergänzen Sie.

1. We got tired _of_ going to the same place every year.
2. You're very good ______ explaining things.
3. The city is famous ______ its museums.
4. But it's always crowded ______ tourists.
5. What are you interested ______?

109 A, B, C or D?

Markieren Sie die richtige Antwort.

1. Who do you know here ... Alice?
   a. apart from b. beside c. except d. next to
2. We live ... Hamburg.
   a. by b. in the near of c. near d. nearby
3. I have no intention ... letting you go off with all our know-how.
   a. at b. for c. of d. on
4. What's the point ... arguing?
   a. at b. in c. on d. to
5. I'm really very proud ... you.
   a. at b. in c. of d. on
6. They accused me ... stealing the code.
   a. at b. for c. from d. of
7. I'll let you know well ... advance.
   a. at b. by c. in d. on
8. We've sold way ... what had been forecast.
   a. ahead b. beyond c. more d. up

15. Dies und das

110 Relative clauses

Kreuzen Sie alle richtigen Lösungen an.

1. Who is the guy ...?
   - a. I saw you with
   - b. that I saw you with
   - c. which I saw you with
   - d. who I saw you with

2. 2 300 were sold, ... were later returned.
   - a. 110 of that
   - b. 110 of which
   - c. of that 110
   - d. 110 of those

3. The teacher ... class gets the best exam results wins an award.
   - a. of who
   - b. of who's
   - c. who's
   - d. whose

111 A or B?

Was stimmt: a oder b?

1. a) I used to live in Frankfurt.
   b) I used to living in Frankfurt.

2. a) He didn't use to have a beard, did he?
   b) He didn't use to having a beard, did he?

3. a) He claimed kids these days are not used to work hard.
   b) He claimed kids these days are not used to working hard.

4. a) I'm slowly getting used to get up at 4.
   b) I'm slowly getting used to getting up at 4.

112 Indirect speech

Wandeln Sie wie im Beispiel um.

1. "Teresa called."
   Raymond told me that Teresa *called / had called* ________________.
2. "We won't have time."
   Jacob insisted that ________________.
3. "I'm leaving tomorrow."
   On Saturday she said that ________________.
4. "Please take a seat."
   She asked me ________________.
5. "Has Rebecca been invited?"
   Tony wanted to know ________________.
6. "Do you speak Portuguese?"
   They asked me ________________.
7. "I'm so excited."
   He said that ________________.
8. "They aren't expecting us."
   Sheila was worried that ________________.
9. "I've made a mistake."
   He knew that ________________.
10. "Will James be there?"
    She wondered ________________.

15

113 A, B or C?

Markieren Sie die richtige Antwort.

1. We're ... outside the station.
   a. meeting b. meeting ourselves c. meeting us
2. They've known ... for a very long time. *[sich]*
   a. each other b. them c. themselves
3. I'd like to introduce ... .
   a. I b. me c. myself
4. Do you have your passport with ...?
   a. you b. your c. yourself
5. Quiet! I can't ... .
   a. concentrate b. concentrate me c. concentrate myself
6. I heard footsteps behind ... .
   a. I b. me c. myself
7. Everyone will have to look after ... . *[sich selbst]*
   a. him and her b. themself c. themselves

114 A or B?

Was stimmt: a oder b?

1. The company has lost most of (a.) it's / (b.) its customers.
2. This suitcase seems to have lost (a.) it's / (b.) its owner.
3. Oh no, (a.) it's / (b.) its raining again.
4. I don't think (a.) it's / (b.) its a pity.
5. What can you tell me about the building and (a.) it's / (b.) its history?
6. I feel (a.) it's / (b.) its time to finish.

Wortschatz und Sprachgebrauch – True and False Friends

16. True friends?

Englisch-deutsche Wortpaare mit ähnlicher Form und Bedeutung – aber nicht immer!

115 I'll take you. *bringen / bring*

Was passt zusammen? Ordnen Sie zu.

1. I'll take you → c.
2. Can you put
3. Can you bring me
4. I don't want to get you
5. First get the children

a. into difficulties.
b. a cloth, please?
c. to the station.
d. to safety.
e. the children to bed?

Und nun ergänzen Sie *bring* oder *take*.

6. We use ________ for a movement away from the person who is speaking.
7. We use ________ for a movement towards the person who is speaking.

116 What a day! *bringen / bring*

Ergänzen Sie passende Übersetzungen von „bringen" aus Übung 115.

What a day! I've been on the go for about 14 hours, non-stop. In the morning they (1.) *brought* our new fitted kitchen. Of course there were problems, with pieces missing and pieces that didn't fit, which really (2.) ________ the workmen into difficulties. The whole thing took longer than expected, and two of them had to go off to another job while the third one finished off. I (3.) ________ him to the bus-stop half an hour ago – not my job I know, but he had such a lot of stuff to carry and had really done a good job, so I took pity on him. In between making tea for the workmen and picking up the kids from school and trying to prepare the presentation I'm giving in Berlin next week, I had to (4.) ________ Julian to the airport. He's gone to Stockholm for a week, on business. I told him not to forget to (5.) ________ something back for the kids. Yes, the kids. It's 9.15, and I've only just (6.) ________ them to bed.

117 Are you coming? *kommen / come*

Welcher Ausdruck passt in die Lücke?

1. A group of us are going to the pub. Are you ...?
   a. coming with b. coming c. by us d. with us
2. Excuse me. How do I ... to the station?
   a. come b. arrive c. get d. reach
3. His temperature is really high. I'm going to ... the doctor.
   a. ask to come b. get to come c. let come d. send for
4. The sender's address ... in the top right-hand corner.
   a. comes b. is belonging c. goes d. places
5. Where do the wine glasses ...? In this cupboard, or in the cupboard in the other room?
   a. come to b. come c. go d. stay
6. We had a very long discussion, but I'm afraid we ... far.
   a. didn't come b. didn't cover c. didn't get d. didn't reach
7. Christmas ... soon.
   a. comes b. is arriving c. is going to be d. will be here
8. Regina ... hospital next week for an operation.
   a. is coming into b. is going to c. comes to the
   d. will be coming into
9. I've put on over six kilos. That ... eating too much and getting too little exercise.
   a. is because b. comes from c. comes of d. goes from

1	2	3	4	5	6	7	8	9
b								

118 I'm looking for … *Karte / card*

Ergänzen Sie eine passende Entsprechung für „Karte".

1. At a kiosk

◆ Yes, please?

● I'm looking for a __________ of the south of England. Not just a plan of London, but the whole of the south of the country.

2. At a restaurant

◆ Was everything all right?

● Yes, it was very nice, thank you.

◆ Would you like a dessert?

● Yes, can we see the __________ again, please?

3. At a theatre booking office

◆ Yes, please?

● I would like three __________s for tomorrow evening's performance, please.

4. In a shop

◆ Isn't it Anna's birthday next week?

● Yes. I must get her a __________.

5. At a station

◆ Excuse me, can you help me with this machine? I want to buy a __________ to go to the city centre.

● That's Zone A. Just press this button here.

119 Coming and going *gehen / go*

Wählen Sie die richtige(n) Lösung(en), um die Übersetzung zu vervollständigen.

1. Es ist nicht weit, ich gehe zu Fuß.
   It's not far, I'm going ... .
   - *(kein weiteres Wort)*
   - by foot
   - to walk

2. Wie lange geht die Sendung?
   How long does the programme ...?
   - go
   - last
   - take

3. Wo gehen die Kinder zur Schule?
   Where do the children ...?
   - go to school
   - go in school
   - walk to school

4. Die Heizung geht nicht.
   The heating ... .
   - doesn't go
   - doesn't function
   - isn't working

5. Wann geht Ihre Maschine?
   When ...?
   - is your flight
   - does your plane go
   - does your flight go

6. Geht der Bus auch sonntags?
   Does the bus ... on Sundays too?
   - drive
   - run
   - travel

7. Das kommt nicht in Frage. Das geht nicht.
   That's out of the question. ...
   - That's not going.
   - That's impossible.
   - I can't make it.

120 Oh damn! *vergessen / forget*

Welches Verb ist richtig?

1. ... the name of the street.
   a. He's forgotten b. He's left

2. ... the piece of paper with the address on at home!
   a. He's forgotten b. He's left

3. Jack is impossible! ... his PIN again!
   a. He's forgotten b. He's left

4. Oh no! ... my mobile in the car!
   a. I've forgotten b. I've left

5. There's big trouble. Williams ... the CD with all the data on the train!
   a. has forgotten b. has left

121 What is it? *Glas / glass*

Ergänzen Sie. Sie können die angegebenen Wörter mehrmals verwenden.

glass • honey • jar • of • olives • wine

1. a ______________________

2. a ______________________

3. a ______________________

4. a ______________________

122 A crossword *Salat, Soße / salad, sauce*

Ergänzen Sie passende Übersetzungen von „Salat" und „Soße" und lösen Sie das Kreuzworträtel.

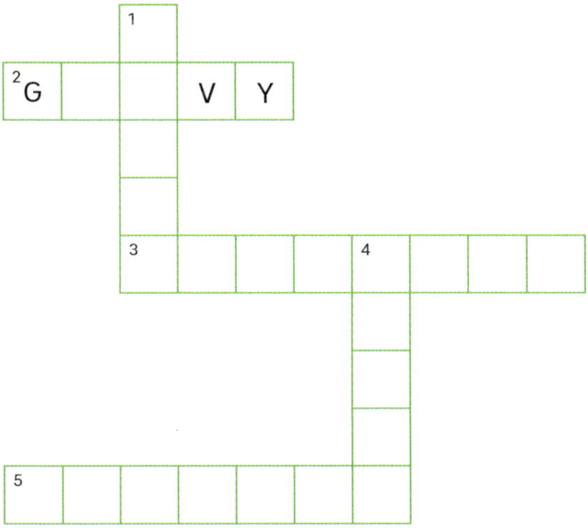

1. This dish is served with French fries and vegetables, or French fries and ... . You can help yourself from the ... bar.
2. I never make ... out of a packet, I always use the meat juices from cooking.
3. What sort of ... do you want on your salad? Italian or French?
4. One of my favourite desserts is ice cream with chocolate ... .
5. We grow our own ... in the garden.

123 In the kitchen *scharf / sharp*

Ergänzen Sie passende Übersetzungen von „scharf".

1. One of the most important pieces of kitchen equipment is a set of ____________ knives.
2. Glenn likes ____________ food – curries, anything with chili powder or Tabasco sauce!

124 Definitions *Gast / guest*

Ordnen Sie zu. Begriffe können mehrmals vorkommen.

customer • guest • guesthouse • host • inn
passenger • visitor

1. When you visit someone in their home, you are that person's ______________.
2. They are your ______________.
3. If they have a room especially for people who come and stay overnight, that is their ______________ room.
4. When you eat in a restaurant, you are one of the restaurant's ______________s.
5. When you stay in a hotel, you are a hotel ______________.
6. When you spend some time in another country, you are a ______________ to that country.
7. When you travel in a taxi, you are the taxi driver's ______________.
8. The place where you go for a drink or a meal with friends, and where you can also stay the night is called an ______________.
9. A ______________ is a sort of small private hotel.

125 Life-long learning *lernen / learn*

Korrigieren Sie – falls nötig!

1. I've decided that I'm going to *learn* ____________ Spanish.
2. Angela is upstairs in her room *learning* ____________. She has a history test tomorrow.
3. Some people just never *learn* ____________ .

126 The test was easy *falsch / false*

Ergänzen Sie *false* oder *wrong*.

1. The test was easy, it consisted of just twenty true-__________ questions.
2. I'm sorry, but your answer is __________.
3. There's no need to worry, it was a __________ alarm.
4. I went to the __________ address.
5. The man gave the police a __________ address, but they soon found out.
6. I only got one question __________, all my other answers were correct.
7. The driver of the other car was on the __________ side of the road. That's why the accident happened.
8. I couldn't understand what I had done __________.
9. I felt such a fool. I had arrived on the __________ day!
10. This class is one for real beginners. If you already know some English, you should register for the __________ beginners' class.

127 Time for coffee *Pause / pause*

Übersetzen Sie.

1. Um 15.00 Uhr machen wir eine Kaffeepause.
   We'll ______________________________ at three o'clock.
2. Es gab eine kurze Pause, nicht mehr als zwei Sekunden.
   ______________________________, not more than two seconds.
3. Das Theaterstück war sehr lang und es gab zwei Pausen.
   ____
4. An manchen Tagen habe ich so viel zu tun, dass ich keine Mittagspause mache.
   ____
5. Die [Schul-]Pause ist nach der zweiten [Unterrichts-]Stunde.
   ____

128 A visit to a castle *dick / thick*

Was ist richtig: a oder b? Oder sind a und b beide richtig?

The castle was really impressive[1], with walls nearly three metres (a.) fat / (b.) thick (1.). One of the most interesting things about it was that it had a library, with some beautiful old leather books, really (a.) fat / (b.) thick (2.) books that must have been very valuable.

We had just finished our tour and were just coming out of the front gate, when a (a.) big fat / (b.) thick (3.) car drove up. It stopped, and a man got out. He was small, but incredibly[2] (a.) fat / (b.) thick (4.). He walked round to the other side of the car, opened the door, and a woman got out. 'Welcome to Wellesborne', he said, and gave her a (a.) big / (b.) thick (5.) kiss on her cheek. She didn't like this at all, it was clearly a (a.) big / (b.) thick (6.) mistake. But it didn't seem to bother him. He laughed and said something to the gatekeeper[3], who then laughed too. They were obviously (a.) close / (b.) thick (7.) friends.

1	2	3	4	5	6	7

[1] beeindruckend
[2] unglaublich
[3] Pförtner/in

129 Some things are extra *extra / extra*

Übersetzen Sie. Verwenden Sie die angegebenen Ausdrücke.

extra • on purpose • separately • specially

1. Kostet das extra?

   ____

2. Ich bezahle den Wein extra.

   ____

3. Ich habe den Wein extra für dich gekauft.

   ____

4. Er hat es extra gemacht, ich bin sicher!

   ____

130 Not long, but … *lang / long*

Ergänzen Sie. Nicht alle angegebenen Wörter werden benötigt und sie können auch mehrfach verwendet werden.

a long time • for • length • long • twenty years

1. I waited ______________, it was almost an hour.
2. ______________ they've been going to the same place for their holidays, every year the same.
3. It was the shoulder-__________ hair that made me think it was a woman.
4. The journey time is the same __________, whether you go by car or by train.
5. I haven't seen them for ______________, it must be over five years since we last met.

131 Young athletes *Preis / price, prize*

Was ist richtig: a oder b?

Some of these gymnasts are very young, not more than 14 or 15 years old. They may win a lot of (a.) prices / (b.) prizes (1.), but they pay a high (a.) price / (b.) prize (2.).

132 Ears open *(zu)hören / hear*

Ergänzen Sie die passende Form von *hear* oder *listen (to)*.

1. ___________ you ___________ the latest news? Another bank is in trouble.
2. I'm sorry, can you say that again? I'm afraid I wasn't ______________________.
3. The train was full, but I just closed my eyes and ______________________ music on my phone.
4. They were shouting at each other. I should think the whole house could ______________________ them.
5. I don't know how many times I've told him not to park outside our gate, but he just won't ______________________!
6. ______________________ closely, and you'll ______________________ the difference.

133 Is it true? *sagen / say*

Ergänzen Sie *say* oder *tell*.

1. Will you please __________ me the truth.
2. Can you __________ me the way to the station?
3. Can you __________ that again, please?
4. __________ hello.
5. I'll __________ them where they can park.
6. __________ us that joke about the DJ again.

134 What people say *sagen / say*

Übersetzen Sie.

1. Können Sie mir sagen, was es kostet?

   ____

2. Ich sage immer die Wahrheit.

   ____

3. Sie sagte *Happy birthday,* aber es war nicht mein Geburtstag.

   ____

4. Sie ist eine sehr stille Person. Sie sagt nicht viel.

   ____

5. Was hat er euch gesagt?

   ____

6. Was hat er gesagt?

   ____

7. Er sagte, er könnte uns nichts sagen.

   ____

8. Das [Fußball-]Spiel war langweilig. – Das kannst du laut sagen!

   ____

135 Everything under control *Kontrolle / control*

Ergänzen Sie passende Übersetzungen von „kontrollieren/Kontrolle“.

1. He was driving too fast and lost __________ of the car on a bend.
2. Remember to pack the scissors in your suitcase. If you put them in your hand luggage, they'll take them away when you get to the security __________.
3. I work in the quality __________ department.
4. It's all right, there's no need to worry. I have everything under __________.
5. We travelled over 300 kilometres and our tickets were not __________ once.
6. Our work is __________ all the time – it's like working in a police state!
7. The authorities[1] carry out random __________s of restaurants to ensure[2] that health standards are maintained[3].

136 Entertaining a visitor *Koch, kochen / cook*

Drei der *kursiv* gedruckten Ausdrücke sind falsch. Korrigieren Sie sie.

◆ Come in, then we can carry on talking while I (1.) *cook* __________ us some tea.

● You have a very nice (2.) *kitchen* __________. I like all this wood.

◆ Thank you.

● Do you (3.) *do much cooking* __________?

◆ No, I don't have time. Brian is the (4.) *cook* __________ in this house. Well, most of the time. At any rate, he gets home first, so he normally (5.) *cooks* __________ our evening meal.

● People always say that English (6.) *kitchen* __________ is not very good. But I don't agree. I've always found that ...

◆ Oh, the water (7.) *is cooking* __________. Excuse me a moment.

[1] Behörden
[2] sicherstellen
[3] eingehalten werden

137 A question of how you feel *warm / warm*

Ergänzen Sie *warm* oder *hot*.

1. a nice ______ day in spring

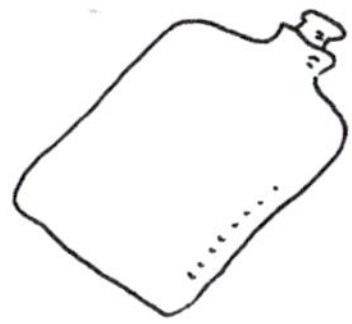

2. a ______- water bottle

3. a ______ meal

4. a terribly ______ day

5. ______ and cold water

6. a nice ______ bath

138 A breath of fresh air *frisch / fresh*

Ergänzen Sie.

bright • clean • chilly • fresh • wet

1. I need to get some __________ air.
2. We sat outside till ten in the evening, but then it got quite __________ and so we went inside.
3. After a day's hard work it's good to have a shower and put on some __________ clothes.
4. The place was decorated in nice __________ colours.
5. Careful! __________ paint!

139 The minimum *null / nil*

Ergänzen Sie.

nil • nought • oh • zero

1. It was a hard-fought match which neither team deserved to lose, so it was right that it finished __________ __________.
2. We had the first frost of the winter last night, the temperature is now just one degree above __________.
3. She broke the world record, but only by point __________ one (0,01) of a second!
4. My mobile number is __________ one five seven, ...
5. In a recession the rate of economic growth drops below __________.

140 Josh's accident *nächste(r/s), neu / next, new*

Ergänzen Sie passende Wörter.

◆ Have you heard the (1.) __________ news?

● No, why? What's happened?

◆ Josh has crashed his (2.) __________ car.

● But he only got it last week.

◆ I know. It was the very (3.) __________ model and must have cost him I don't know how much.

● How did it happen?

◆ Someone stopped him and asked the way to the (4.) __________ bank, so he said, "I'll drive you there, it's only just round the corner." And it was, just round the corner, but they didn't get there because Josh overlooked a red light.

● (5.) __________ time he'll know better than to show off to strangers.

141 More on cars *Motor / motor*

Wählen Sie die richtige Lösung, a oder b.

We had a terrible journey back from Scotland. It was raining, but the windscreen wipers weren't working properly. There was something wrong with the electric (a.) engine / (b.) motor (1.). We stopped and got that repaired, but then in the middle of a wild stretch of countryside the car broke down completely. This time, it was something major to do with the (a.) engine / (b.) motor (2.).

1	2

142 All the latest *Technik / technique*

Ergänzen Sie *technique* oder *technology*.

1. In this course you will learn an important marketing ______________.
2. There have been huge advances in medical ____________ over the last 50 years.
3. Roberta has a new trainer, and her ______________ has improved enormously. She's developing into a first-class player.
4. The company fell behind because it didn't invest in new ____________.

143 Light and dark *Schatten / shade, shadow*

Was ist richtig: a oder b?

1. It's too hot in the sun. Let's try and find a table in the (a.) shade / (b.) shadow.
2. As the sun began to go down behind us, our (a.) shades / (b.) shadows on the lawn grew longer and longer.
3. The news of Will's heart attack cast[1] a (a.) shade / (b.) shadow over the whole evening.
4. He's now only a (a.) shade / (b.) shadow of the man he used to be.
5. After lunch, I lay down and slept in the (a.) shade / (b.) shadow of a big chestnut tree[2].

1	2	3	4	5

[1] warf
[2] Kastanienbaum

144 And so to bed *schlafen / sleep*

Was ist richtig: a oder b? Oder sind a und b beide richtig?

1. Sleep researchers have found that we now (a.) are asleep / (b.) sleep over an hour less than fifty years ago.
2. Fifty years ago people were often in bed and (a.) asleep / (b.) sleeping by ten thirty in the evening.
3. It's been a long day and I think it's time for me to go to (a.) bed / (b.) sleep. Goodnight everybody and thanks for a wonderful evening.
4. I'm sorry I disturbed you. I didn't realize you were (a.) asleep / (b.) sleeping.
5. Most nights I switch the light off and (a.) am asleep / (b.) sleep within ten minutes.
6. Sometimes I wake in the middle of the night and have problems (a.) getting back to sleep / (b.) falling asleep again.
7. I'm not one of these people who sleep (a.) in / (b.) late at the weekend. I still get up quite early.
8. The presentation was so boring, the speaker's voice so monotonous that it (a.) brought / (b.) sent me to sleep.

1	2	3	4	5	6	7	8

145 Opinion poll results *Politik / politics, policy*

Ergänzen Sie *politics, policy* oder *policies.*

1. In the opinion poll, over 30% of young people said they weren't interested in ______________.
2. In the same poll, over 50% of all respondents said they were dissatisfied with the government's economic ______________.
3. As always, the US presidential election seems to be more about personalities. It's not clear what ______________ each candidate has on the major issues facing the country.

146 In the media *Programm / programme, program*

Übersetzen Sie.

1. Sie hatten kein Satellitenfernsehen und es gab nur drei Programme.

   ____

2. Es gibt viele Verbesserungen in der neuen Version des [Computer-] Programms.

   ____

3. Das Festivalprogramm ist nun erschienen.

   ____

4. Welches [TV-]Programm schauen Sie am meisten?

   ____

147 Not always a house *Haus / house*

Korrigieren Sie – falls nötig!

1. I'm sorry, but Herr Werner is out of the *house* ______________. Try calling back this afternoon.
2. Ann and Steve have just sold their *house* ______________.
3. The hospital always sends a report to your *house doctor* ______________.
4. The teacher gives a lot of work to be done at *house* ______________.

148 What do you mean? *meinen / mean*

Korrigieren Sie – falls nötig.

1. What do you *mean* by ________________ "very expensive"?
2. When I said, "he's too old", I *didn't mean* ________________ you.
3. I *mean* ____________ it's a good idea. What's your view?
4. I'm sorry. I *didn't mean* ______________ to hurt you.
5. I agree with you entirely. I *mean* _____________ exactly the same.

149 Getting it right *Komma / comma*

Ergänzen Sie eine passende Übersetzung von „Komma".

1. The increase was minimal, just nought ________________ seven per cent.
2. In German you always put a _____________ before *dass*, but in English you never put one before "that".

150 What do you want? *wollen / want*

Welche Verbform ist richtig?

1. We got to the station just as the train ... leave.
   a. wanted to   b. was about to
2. Lots of migrants ... America.
   a. want to   b. want to get to
3. Damn! The car ... start.
   a. doesn't want to   b. won't
4. There we were, ready to leave, and the car ... start.
   a. didn't want to   b. wouldn't

1	2	3	4

151 I want to go *wollen / want*

Übersetzen Sie.

1. Wen wollen Sie sprechen?

   ____

2. Ich wollte gerade gehen, als Jim anrief.

   ____

3. Der Besucher will zu Mr Smith.

   ____

4. Ich will ins Bett.

   ____

5. Ich hab's ihr hundert Mal gesagt, aber sie will einfach nicht hören.
   I've told her a hundred times, but ______________________________

6. Ich versuchte das Fenster zu öffnen, aber es wollte nicht.

   ____

7. Moment mal! Was wollen Sie damit sagen?! Dass ich ein Dieb bin?!
   Just a moment! ____________________? That I'm a thief?!

8. Wir könnten ins Theater gehen, wenn du willst.

   ____

152 Your money *Kosten, kosten / cost(s)*

Ergänzen Sie passende Übersetzungen von „kosten/Kosten".

1. The ___________ of petrol rose last year by over 15%.
2. Will we save on production ___________ by introducing the new technology? That's the key question.
3. The ___________ of living in London will be a real shock for them when they move there.
4. It will ___________ too much time. We'll have to drop the idea.
5. Money doesn't seem to be a problem. He wants to go so much that he's prepared to go at his own ___________.
6. How much will it ___________ to park at the airport?

153 Help! *helfen / help*

Ergänzen Sie die Übersetzung. Verwenden Sie die vorgegebenen Wörter.

It's • do • for • good • is • no • one • only
There's • thing • to • use

1. Es hilft nichts. Wir müssen ganz von vorne anfangen.
   ______________________. We're going to have to start all over again.
2. Honig mit Zitrone hilft gegen Halsschmerzen.
   Honey with lemon ______________________ a sore throat.
3. Da hilft nur eins: alle Banken verstaatlichen.
   ______________________: nationalize all the banks.

154 Lots of people *Publikum, publik / public*

Ist das *kursiv* gesetzte Wort richtig oder falsch?

1. It's an absolute scandal. This needs to be made *public*.

2. At the end of the play the *public* gave the actors a standing ovation.

155 It's natural *Natur / nature*

Ergänzen Sie die Übersetzungen.

1. Am Wochenende bin ich gern in der freien Natur.
   At the weekend I like to be out in the ________________.

2. Es liegt in der menschlichen Natur, Fehler zu machen.
   It's h________ __________ to make mistakes.

3. Pflanzen, Tiere, Menschen: wir alle sind Teil der Natur.
   Plants, animals, human beings: we are all part of ____________.

156 Is it OK? *wenn / when*

Ergänzen Sie *when* oder *if*.

1. Is it OK _________ we meet a little bit later?
2. We can discuss everything else _________ we meet.
3. I'll let you know _________ the flight arrives.
4. _________ you need any help, just ask.
5. _________ things continue like this, we'll have to take drastic action.
6. I'll only phone _________ there's a problem.
7. Start without us _________ we're late. Don't wait.
8. _________ we finish, I'll take them on a guided tour.
9. _________ we finish early, I'll fill in time by taking them on a guided tour.

157 Enjoy yur meal *Menü, grillen / menu, barbecue*

Kreuzen Sie alle korrekten Sätze an.

1. a. I'll have today's menu, please.
   b. I'll have today's special, please.
   c. I'll have today's set meal, please.

2. a. Here you are, sir. Enjoy your meal.
   b. Here you are, sir. Bon appétit.
   c. Here you are, sir. Good appetite.

3. a. It's a beautiful evening for a grill.
   b. It's a beautiful evening for a barbecue.
   c. It's a beautiful evening to grill.
   d. It's a beautiful evening to have a grill party.

158 Plans and activities *Aktion / action*

Welcher Ausdruck passt in die Lücke?

1. Which products are we going to place at the centre of our summer advertising ...?
   a. action b. campaign
2. We already have a provisional plan of ... .
   a. action b. campaign
3. There has been more military ... in Northern Afghanistan.
   a. action b. campaign
4. A number of different charities have launched ... to help the victims of the earthquake.
   a. an action b. a campaign

159 Criminal activity *rauben / rob*

Kreuzen Sie die richtige Lösung an.

	rob	steal	
1.	*X*		a bank
2.			jewels from someone's house
3.			priceless paintings from a museum
4.			somebody on the underground
5.			a team of what seemed certain victory
6.			a film star of her diamond ring
7.			the tomb of an Egyptian king
8.			stationery from the office
9.			13 million from an online bank account
10.			people of their life savings

160 Not always high *hoch / high*

Übersetzen Sie.

1. Es war kalt und wir hatten hohen Schnee.
2. Santa Claus wohnt im hohen Norden.
3. Es war Hochsommer und das Gras war hoch.
4. Wie hoch war der Betrag, der gestohlen wurde?
5. Sie hat eine hoch bezahlte Stelle bei einer Computerfirma.
6. Die Stadt ist von hohen Bergen umgeben.
7. Hände hoch!
8. Der Zug fuhr mit hoher Geschwindigkeit in den Tunnel hinein.
9. Wir rechnen mit nicht mehr als 30 Personen, wenn es hoch kommt.
10. Immer mehr Menschen erreichen ein hohes Alter.
11. Er hat hohe Schulden.
12. Die Mannschaft hat hoch gewonnen.

161 It's chaos at home. *lassen / let*

Was passt in die Lücke? Mehrere Lösungen sind möglich.

1. It's chaos at home.
   We ... the whole house ...
   a. are letting ... repaint
   b. are letting ... repainted
   c. are having ... repainted
   d. are making ... repainted

2. I'm a bit short of time.
   ... to explain it to you.
   a. Let Wanda
   b. Get Wanda
   c. Ask Wanda
   d. Make Wanda

3. They ... over half an hour.
   a. kept us waiting
   b. made us wait
   c. let us to wait
   d. made us to wait

4. ...! You know I don't like it.
   a. Let that
   b. Leave that
   c. Let that be
   d. Stop that

5. Can you just ..., please?!
   a. let me
   b. leave me alone
   c. leave me to be
   d. leave me work

6. Can you ... for everyone, please?
   a. let copies make
   b. have copies made
   c. make copies to be made
   d. make it be copied

Und nun übersetzen Sie.

7. Robin und Ann lassen euch grüßen.

___

162 On the road *Straße / street*

Ergänzen Sie *road* oder *street*.

1. a ____________________

2. a ____________________

3. A ____________ is what cars, buses etc. use to get from A to B.
4. A ____________ is a place where people live, work, go shopping, etc.

163 These city streets *Straße / street*

Kreuzen Sie die richtige Lösung an.

	road	street	
1.	○	○	Excuse me. Is this the ... to Inverness?
2.	○	○	How much crime is there? How safe are the ...s in this part of town?
3.	○	○	The private detective stood on the ... corner reading a newspaper.
4.	○	○	Drivers need to take extra care on the ...s this morning. There is a lot of fog about.
5.	○	○	He was driving far too fast and came off the ... .
6.	○	○	The country ... is best if you want to enjoy the scenery.
7.	○	○	The exhibition centre is on the ... to Walsall.
8.	○	○	The major shopping ...s are to the west of the station.

164 Welcome to Wembley … *Stadium / stadium*

Was passt in die Lücke?

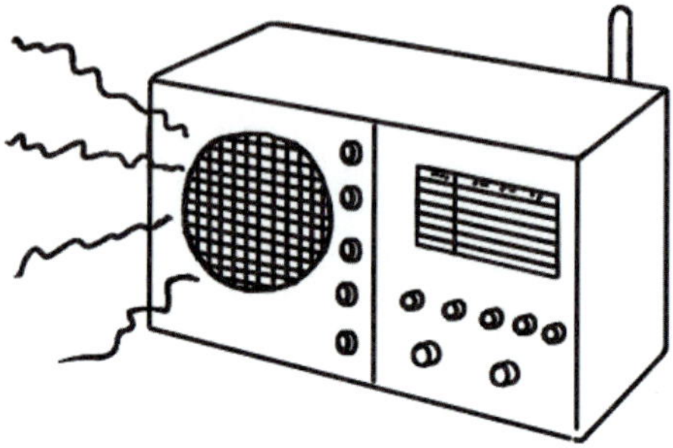

Welcome back to Wembley (1.) …, where the second half of this important qualifying match is already well under way. At this (2.) … of the game, ten minutes into the second half, the match is wide open, and either team could win.

1. a. sports centre c. stadion
   b. sports ground d. stadium

2. a. part c. segment
   b. event d. stage

165 Make and do *machen / make*

Kreuzen Sie die richtige Lösung an.

	make	do	
1.	○	○	I can't ... this sudoku. Can you help me?
2.	○	○	What am I to ...? I've tried everything.
3.	○	○	Do you have to ... much overtime in your job?
4.	○	○	We need to ... some decisions.
5.	○	○	If I cook, will you ... the washing up?
6.	○	○	I'm afraid I'm going to ... a mistake.
7.	○	○	I'll ... the shopping on my way home.
8.	○	○	Does it ... any difference what I think?
9.	○	○	What do you ... for a living?
10.	○	○	I'd like to ... a Chinese course.
11.	○	○	I used to ... quite a lot of sport.
12.	○	○	I'd like to ... a suggestion if I may.

166 Don't worry. *machen / make*

Übersetzen Sie.

1. Wann machen Sie in diesem Jahr Urlaub?

   ____

2. Warte, ich will ein Foto machen.

   ____

3. Es macht nichts.

   ____

4. Sollen wir Pause machen?

   ____

5. Ich mache Diät.

   ____

6. Wann machen Sie Ihre Prüfung?

   ____

7. Mach dir keine Sorgen.

   ____

167 Let's make this work! *machen / make*

Ergänzen Sie die richtige(n) Verbform(en).

1. The engine ... a funny noise. Let's should stop and see what's wrong.
   - is doing
   - is making
2. In German dogs ... *wau wau*, but in English 'woof woof'.
   - do
   - go
   - make
3. On Sunday afternoons we always had to ... a walk. It was awful.
   - do
   - go for
   - make
4. I only ... four questions right.
   - did
   - got
   - made
5. It's not ideal, but let's ... the best of it.
   - do
   - make
6. I'm ... my best.
   - doing
   - making
7. Let's ... a start, we have a lot to get through.
   - do
   - get
   - make
8. Can you ... me a favour?
   - do
   - give
   - make
9. Quite a number of employees ... a little sleep during the lunch break.
   - do
   - have
   - make
10. You've ... a really good job. Thank you very much indeed.
    - done
    - made
11. At school I used to like ... translations.
    - doing
    - making

17. False friends

Englisch-deutsche Wortpaare mit ähnlicher Form aber unterschiedlicher Bedeutung

168 Globalization *Fabrik / fabric*

Kreuzen Sie die richtige(n) Antwort(en) an.

The company I used to work for produces (1.) ... for the furniture industry, for sofas, beds, etc. They used to have (2.) ... in western Europe, but now most of the production is based in Rumania. When the company relocated, many people lost their jobs.

1. a. cloths c. materials
   b. fabrics d. stuffs

2. a. fabrics c. production places
   b. factories d. workplaces

169 What makes a good film? *Kritik / critic*

Richtig oder falsch? Wenn falsch, wie lautet der richtige Ausdruck?

◆ Did you enjoy the film?
● I did. Films that have a (1.) *happy end* _happy ending_ make you feel good.
◆ That doesn't mean they are good films.
● You sound like one of these film (2.) *critics* ___________. Anyway. Have you read the (3.) *critic* ___________ of the film in the paper?

170 Please fill it in. *Formular / formula*

Ergänzen Sie *form* oder *formula*.

1. Can you please fill in this ___________?
2. What is your ___________ for success?
3. This weekend is the last race in this year's ___________ One series.
4. What's the mathematical ___________ for calculating the area of a circle?
5. Support in the ___________ of cash is also very welcome.

171 In a café *überhören / overhear*

Was passt in die Lücke? Mehrere Lösungen sind möglich.

As I was sitting in the café waiting for Minako, I (1.) ... two men at the next table talking about a "delivery at midnight", and I thought I heard the word 'cocaine'. I tried to catch what else they were saying. I was listening so intently to their conversation that I (2.) ... my mobile ringing. It was Minako calling to say she'd be late.

1. a. became with c. overheard
   b. happened to hear d. overcame
2. a. didn't hear c. heard over
   b. failed to hear d. overheard

172 Times are changing *Chef, Personal / boss, staff ...*

Ergänzen Sie. Jede Linie steht für einen Buchstaben.

1. Banks used to have b *r a n c h e* s in every town.
2. Companies in our b _ _ _ _ _ _ s are really feeling the recession.
3. There has been another big t _ _ _ _ _ _ _. The second biggest bank in the country has bought up the fourth biggest.
4. We were going so slowly that even people on bikes o _ _ _ _ _ _ k us!
5. The company has been forced to cut costs and reduce s _ _ _ _.
6. PIN stands for _ _ _ _ _ _ _ _ identification number.
7. A firm that organizes funerals is called an u _ _ _ _ _ _ _ _ _.
8. Bill Gates must be seen as one of the great ent _ _ pre _ _ _ _s of the 20th century.
9. How are you getting on with your new b _ _ _?
10. A _ _ _ _ works in a restaurant and plans and cooks meals.

17

173 Don't just sit there! *Rückseite / backside*

Was passt in die Lücke? Mehrere Lösungen sind möglich.

Mother	Don't just sit there on your (1.) ...! Get up and do something.
Son	What?
Mother	Well, for a start you can go and get the rest of the shopping out of the car.
Son	Where is it?
Mother	Parked (2.) ... of the building where it always is!

1. a. backside c. bottom
   b. behind d. sit

2. a. at the back side c. on the back side
   b. at the back d. on the back

174 Definitions *selbstbewusst, sensibel / self-confident, sensible*

Ordnen Sie zu.

pleasant • self-conscious • self-confident
sensible • sensitive • sympathetic

1. Someone who is ________________ is often nervous and worries about what other people think of them.
2. A ______________ person is the opposite of the type of person described in sentence 1. This sort of person feels good about him- or herself.
3. A ________________ person is someone who is practical and makes wise decisions.
4. If you are ________________ ,you have good antennae for how other people feel, you can put yourself in their situation and understand how they feel.
5. If you like another person, you find them nice or ______________.
6. A ________________ person listens carefully to your worries and cares about your problems.

175 I prefer people like you and me *ordinär / ordinary*

Was passt in die Lücke? Mehrere Lösungen sind möglich.

Mr Bagshot may have lots of money and lots of friends in high places, but I find him distinctly (1.) … . He's always telling jokes and stories that are in bad taste. I prefer normal, (2.) … people – people like you and me!

1. a. common c. out of the ordinary
   b. orderly d. vulgar

2. a. ordinal c. ordinary
   b. every day d. usual

176 What is what? *Keks / cake*

Ergänzen Sie.

1. a ______________________________

2. a ______________________________

177 What do you think? *Meinung / meaning*

Korrigieren Sie.

◆ What do you think of the new proposals that have been put forward by the government?

● I'm sceptical. What's your *meaning* ____________?

178 Have you got your results? *Note, Notiz / note, notice*

Ergänzen Sie *note, notice* oder einen anderen passenden Ausdruck.

1. ◆ I hear that you've got your exam results. What ____________ did you get?

   ● An A in English, and a C in German.
2. I have to write a summary of the meeting, but there's one topic where the ____________s I took are not clear.
3. I must make a mental ____________ of that so that I don't forget.
4. When he got home he found a ____________ on the kitchen table saying she was gone.
5. The best thing to do is to ignore him. Just don't take any ____________.
6. There was a big ____________ on the gate saying 'Please do not feed the animals'.
7. I carry a little ____________book round with me in which I write down all the new words I hear. It's a good way to learn new vocabulary.
8. I can sing OK, but I can't read ____________. I have to learn new songs by listening.

179 Things that arrive *bekommen / become*

Welcher Satz ist richtig?

1.

a. I become the quiche, please.
b. I get the quiche, please.
c. I have the quiche, please.
d. I'll have the quiche, please.

2.

a. Fran has become a baby.
b. Fran got a baby.
c. Fran has had a baby.
d. Fran has received a baby.

180 What the postman brings *Paket / packet*

Übersetzen Sie.

1. Wann holt der Kurier die Pakete ab?

____

2. Die Regierung hat ein Maßnahmenpaket bewilligt.
The government has approved _______________

3. Ich benutze mehrere Softwarepakete von Microsoft.

____

4. Zwei Päckchen Butter und ein Päckchen Tee.

____

181 Different concepts *Konzept / concept*

Ist der *kursiv* gedruckte Ausdruck richtig oder falsch? Wenn falsch, korrigieren Sie ihn.

1. The *concept* ____________ of 'democracy' goes back to ancient Greece.
2. I've completed the first *concept* ____________ of my dissertation, but it is still very rough and needs more work done on it.
3. The marketing *concept* ____________ for the new brand includes a whole range of activities and measures.
4. The question completely *brought him out of his concept* ____________________.

182 This and that *Mappe, Tablett, Foto / map, tablet, photo*

Beschriften Sie die Bilder.

folder • map • photograph • photographer • tablet • tray

1. ________________

2. ________________

3. ________________

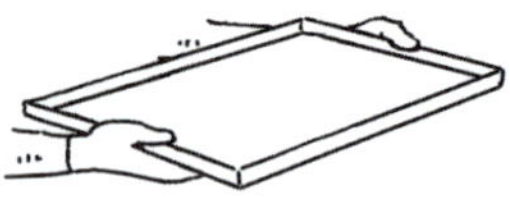

4. ________________

5. ________________

6. ________________

183 Killed by a cup of tea *Mörder, Gift / murder, gift*

Ergänzen Sie.

gift • murder • murderer • poison

Police are investigating the bizarre (1.) ______________ of an old lady in an old people's home. It seems that the (2.) ______________ killed his or her victim by putting some (3.) ______________ into the old lady's early-morning tea. It was her birthday, and she had received a number of cards and (4.) ______________.

184 What's on a piece of paper *Rezept / receipt*

Übersetzen Sie.

1. Ich bezahlte und der Taxifahrer gab mir eine Quittung.

   ____

2. Es schmeckt wunderbar. Du musst mir das Rezept geben.

   ____

3. Das Rezept muss noch von der Ärztin unterschrieben werden.

   ____

4. Was ist Ihr Erfolgsrezept?

   ____

17

185 Hard times *Rente / rent*

Was passt in die Lücke? Mehrere Lösungen sind möglich.

1. More and more old people are finding it hard to survive[1] on the state ... .
   a. pay c. retirement money
   b. pension d. old-age allowance

2. She'll be 66 next March and will be ... .
   a. going to rent c. retiring
   b. going into retirement d. going to rest

3. My flat has become too expensive. My landlord[2] put up the ... again.
   a. monthly fee c. rent
   b money d. tax

[1] überleben
[2] Vermieter

186 Actually, no ... *aktuell / actual*

Ergänzen Sie jeweils die passende Entsprechung von „aktuell".

1. ◆ You can't go by that timetable. It's no longer v __ __ __ __.
   ● Sorry?
   ◆ It's no longer u __ to d __ __ __.

2. ◆ Hunault's latest book is set in the present day and is about the winners and losers of globalization.
   ● So it's very t __ __ __ __ __ __.

3. ◆ What's in the news?
   ● The same thing as last week and the week before. All the media are full of the c __ __ __ __ __ __ crisis in the banking sector.

187 Money matters *sparen, spenden / spare, spend*

Ergänzen Sie (eine passende Form von) *save, spare, spend* oder *donate*.

1. Can you ______________ me ten minutes? I'd like to ask you for some advice.
2. It'll ______________ time and help to keep the meeting short if you arrange it for quite late in the afternoon.
3. I got €300 out of the bank this morning and I've ______________ it all already. I'm not very good at managing my money.
4. When the economic climate cools down, people ______________ less to charity.
5. You can ___________ a few euros if you book online. It's slightly cheaper.

188 An accident *übersehen, Handy / oversee, handy*

Korrigieren Sie.

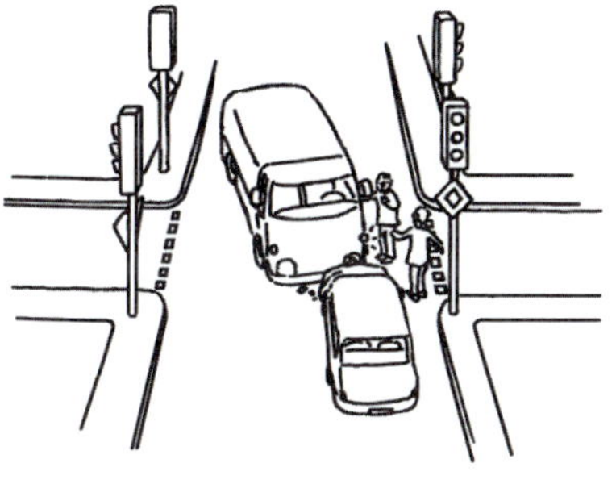

This is how the accident happened. The driver of the delivery van was on his (1.) ~~handy~~ ______________ and not paying attention to what was happening on the road. He wanted to turn left, and had (2.) ~~blinked~~ ______________ left, but he (3.) ~~oversaw~~ ______________ the car coming the other way.

It all happened in the *blink* of an eye, very quickly indeed. There were plenty of other witnesses besides me because I *was overseeing* a group of students who were doing a photography project. It was *handy* that they all had cameras.

189 Children *brav, Gymnasium / brave, gymnasium*

Was passt in die Lücke? Mehrere Lösungen sind möglich.

1. ◆ Our usual babysitter goes to the same school as Tina.
   ● Which school is that?
   ◆ The local …
   a. gymnasium c. grammar school
   b. second school d. higher school

2. ● Is that a good school?
   ◆ Yes, we're very happy. There don't seem to be any problems with … or anything like that.
   a. bullying c. mobbing
   b. harassers d. mobbsters

3. ◆ Has everything been OK?
   ● Yes, the children have been very …, no problem at all. They went to bed when I told them to, did exactly what I asked them to do.
   ◆ They're not like that with us, I can assure you!
   a. brave c. bold
   b. good d. well-behaved

190 Keeping fit *Gymnastik, wandern / gymnastics, wander*

Ergänzen Sie *exercises, gymnastics, hiking* oder *wandering*.
Benutzen Sie jedes Wort nur einmal.

1. ________________ is an Olympic discipline. Some of the best athletes are still children.
2. I'm not one of these people who get out of bed in the morning and do their keep-fit ________________.
3. I had an hour to spare, so I spent it ________________ round the old town.
4. Autumn is the best time to go ________________ in the mountains.

191 The weekend paper *Prospekt, Annonce / prospect, brochure*

Ergänzen Sie.

advertisement • announcements • brochures • prospects

The first thing I do when I get the weekend paper is to sort out and throw away all the bits I'm not interested in. These include all the separate advertising (1.) ____________ and all the (2.) ____________ sections for jobs, housing, cars, etc.
The paper is still then very thick, and my (3.) ____________ of getting through all of it very slim. So another thing I don't read is the section with all the birth, marriage and death (4.) ____________.

192 In the air *gründen / ground*

Ergänzen Sie *founded* oder *grounded*.

British Airways was (1.) ____________ in 1974, when the two companies BOAC (British Overseas Airways Corporation) and BEA (British European Airways) were merged[1]. BOAC had previously been (2.) ____________, when British Airways and Imperial Airways were merged in 1937.
As you can see, today we have thick fog here at the airport, and most of the fleet has been (3.) ____________ .

[1] wurden fusioniert

193 Not now, but … *eventuell / eventually*

Wählen Sie den Ausdruck oder die Ausdrücke mit der gleichen Bedeutung wie *eventually*.

1. The train *eventually* arrived, over 45 minutes late.
   - sometime
   - at last
   - finally
   - one day
2. *Eventually* all this will belong to you, son.
   - sometime
   - at last
   - finally
   - one day

194 Don't wait *eventuell / eventually*

Wählen Sie alle passenden Übersetzungen.

1. Er kommt eventuell nicht. Wir sollen nicht auf ihn warten.
   a. He may not come. We are not to wait for him.
   b. He possibly won't be coming. We are not to wait for him.
   c. It's possible that he won't be coming. We are not to wait for him.
   d. He likely won't be coming. We are not to wait for him.
2. Wir haben eventuell ein Problem.
   a. We can have a problem.
   b. We possibly have a problem.
   c. We may have a problem.
   d. We have a possible problem.

1	2

195 What you need to make something *Stoff / stuff*

Ergänzen Sie die Übersetzungen.

1. Aus welchem Stoff ist das Zelt?
   What ______________ is the tent made of?

2. Ich habe Stoff gekauft und werde die Vorhänge selber nähen.
   I've bought some ______________ and am going to make the curtains myself.

3. Es gibt verschiedene chemische Stoffe, die diese Eigenschaft haben.
   There are various chemical ______________ that have this property.

4. Wo findet sie den Stoff für ihre Geschichten?
   Where does she find the ______________ for her stories?

196 Goods *Warenhaus / warehouse*

Was passt in die Lücken?

Goods are produced, stored in a ... (1.), then moved to the place where they are sold – for example, big ...s (2.), like KDW in Berlin, Macy's in New York, or Selfridges in London.

a. department store
b. shopping store
c. retail house
d. warehouse

197 A question of religion *Konfession / confession*

Ergänzen Sie.

belief • confession • denomination • denotation

◆ What (1.) ______________ are you? Protestant or Roman Catholic?

● Roman Catholic. At least on paper.

◆ So that means you go to (2.) ______________?

● Sorry?

◆ You go to the priest and tell him what you have done wrong.

● Well, I should do, or would do if I was a practising Roman Catholic.

198 Wedding bells *engagiert / engaged*

Sortieren Sie die Buchstaben.

1. Laura and Michael have just got *G A N E G E D* ______________. The wedding is going to take place next March.
2. Laura is a teacher. She's very *T E A D D E D I C* ______________ to her job.
3. Michael is a social worker. He's also very *T E M O M C I T D* ______________ to his work.
4. Both of them are heavily *V O N E V D I L* ______________ in the anti-globalization movement.
5. They are a politically and socially *I V E C A T* ______________ couple.
6. So please don't tell them that I've just been *D E R I H* ______________ by one of the big multi-nationals!

18. Lots of friends

Ein Wort im Deutschen – mehrere im Englischen

199 At a party. *Mann, Frau*

Ergänzen Sie die richtige Übersetzung von „Mann" und „Frau".

1

2

3

4

5

200 Here you are. *bitte*

Was passt zusammen? Ordnen Sie zu.

1. Darf ich mich hierher setzen? – *Bitte schön.* → b
2. Vielen Dank. – *Bitte schön.*
3. *Bitte schön*, Ihr Schlüssel.
4. Kann ich *bitte* das Salz haben?
5. *Wie bitte*? Ich verstehe leider nicht.

a. Here you are, your key.
b. May I sit here? – Certainly. / Of course. / Please do.
c. Thanks very much. – It's a pleasure. / That's all right. / You're welcome.
d. Sorry? / Pardon? / Excuse me? I'm afraid I don't understand.
e. Can I have the salt please?

201 In a German restaurant *bitte*

Ergänzen Sie den Dialog mit passenden Ausdrücken aus Übung 200.

◆ Excuse me. Do you mind if I join you?
● Entschuldigung?
◆ May I sit here?
● Yes, (1.) ______________________. …
◆ Can I see the menu, please?
● *(Gives the menu.)* (2.) ______________________.
◆ Thanks very much.
Hmm. Interesting. But can you explain what this is, 'xzysxwlm'?
● (3.) ______________________?
◆ Sorry, it's my German pronunciation. I can't say it properly.
● Can I see, (4.) ______________________?
◆ Sure. *(Points to something.)* Here.
● Ah, 'Saumagen'. Well, that's something very, er, special, it's …
◆ Thanks for all your help.
● (5.) ______________________.

18

202 A postcard *als*

Ergänzen Sie eine passende Entsprechung für „als".

(1.) ____________ we arrived, it was pouring with rain. And that's how the holiday has continued. I don't think we've had a wetter holiday (2.) __________ this one! When people find out that I'm English, they say, "Well, (3.) __________ an English person you must be used to this." (4.) __________ if it rained all the time in England!

203 Where you go and what you do *besuchen*

Ergänzen Sie eine passende Übersetzung von „besuchen".

attend • go to • visit

1. We're not going away, can't afford a holiday this year. We'll probably take the odd day and go and ____________ friends or relatives.
2. In this country children have to ____________ school until the age of 16.
3. Even if you don't live in the city, you can still enjoy what's on offer culturally, ____________ concerts and things.

204 Payment *(be)zahlen*

Kreuzen Sie die richtige Lösung an.

	pay	pay for	
1.	X	○	taxes
2.	○	○	repairs
3.	○	○	€ 80 for something
4.	○	○	tickets in cash
5.	○	○	€ 18 each for the tickets
6.	○	○	a taxi driver
7.	○	○	a taxi to take someone somewhere
8.	○	○	bills
9.	○	○	a person or an amount of money
10.	○	○	a product or service

205 My grandmother *(sich) erinnern, Gedächtnis, Erinnerung*

Ergänzen Sie.

My grandmother says that her (1.) m _e_ _m_ _o_ _r_ _y_ is failing. Like a lot of older people she can (2.) r _ _ _ _ _ _ _ _ many things from a long time ago, and some of her (3.) m _ _ _ _ _ _ _ are really vivid. But she has problems with her (4.) s _ _ _ _-term m _ _ _ _ _. She goes into the garden, for example, and then can't (5.) r _ _ _ _ _ _ _ what she went for. And she forgets things like doctor's appointments. She needs someone or something to (6.) r _ _ _ _ _ her.

For her last birthday we grandchildren gave her a mobile phone and showed her how to use the organizer function, so that she gets a (7.) r _ _ _ _ _ _ _ when she needs one. But of course she only gets it if she (8.) r _ _ _ _ _ _ _ to switch the mobile on!

18

206 A crossword *gesund*

Ergänzen Sie.

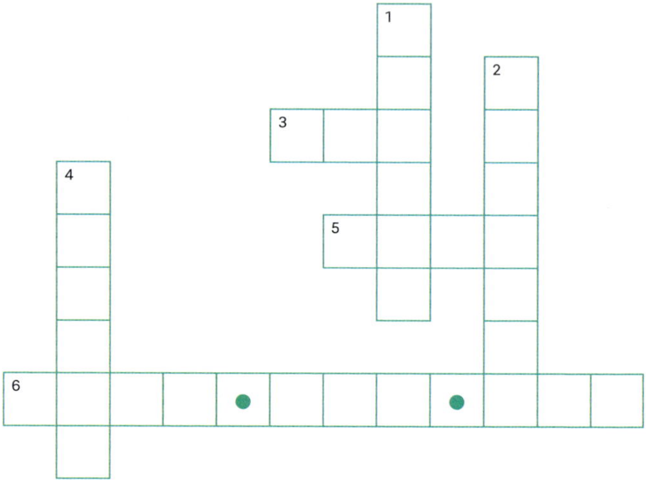

Across

3. My grandmother is still f __ __ and well at the age of 96.
5. I was sorry to hear that you're in hospital. Get w __ __ __ soon!
6. At least there's one thing that the experts seem to agree on – that fruit and vegetables are g __ __ __ f __ __ y __ __.

Down

1. Dave was ill last week, but he's b __ __ __ __ __ again now and back at work.
2. The older you get, the more important it is to adopt a h __ __ __ __ __ __ lifestyle.
4. If you use your c __ __ __ __ __ sense, it's obvious what you should do.

207 More coming and going *fahren*

Welche Form ist richtig?

1. The traffic got so bad that I gave up ... to work. I now commute by train. — a. going b. driving c. travelling
2. Is it difficult to ... a heavy motorbike? — a. drive b. lead c. ride
3. The high-speed trains ... at over 250 km/h. — a. drive b. ride c. travel
4. How often do the trains ... at this time of day? — a. ride b. drive c. run
5. It's OK, I'm going your way. I'll ... home. — a. drive you b. travel you c. bring you
6. In the evenings I usually ... the 6 o'clock train. — a. go with b. take c. ride
7. There was a police radar trap, but I was OK. I was only ... a little over 50 km/h. — a. doing b. driving c. riding
8. If it's wet, I don't walk but ... the bus to work. — a. go with b. take c. ride
9. How fast does this moped ...? — a. drive b. go c. do
10. It was late so we ... . — a. went home with a taxi b. took a taxi home c. drove home with a taxi
11. I ... when I was 17. — a. learned to drive b. made my driving c. did my driving licence

208 People who teach *Lehrer*

Ergänzen Sie *teacher* oder *instructor*.

1. a driving ______________________

2. a school ______________________

3. a riding ______________________

4. a swimming ______________________

5. a university __________, or lecturer

6. People who teach skills are called __________s.
7. People who teach a school or academic subject are called __________s.

209 Not much room *eng*

Ergänzen Sie eine passende Übersetzung von „eng".

close • closely • narrow • tight

1. These trousers are ____________. Have they become smaller in the wash, or have I put on weight?
2. We've been ____________ friends for over 10 years.
3. Be careful, at the bottom of the hill is a ____________ bend.
4. The words *thanks* and *danke* are ____________ related.

210 The right preposition *gegen*

Ergänzen Sie eine passende Entsprechung für „gegen".

1. Es tut mir leid, aber ich kann nichts dagegen tun.
   I'm very sorry, but I can't do anything __________ it.
2. Nehmen Sie etwas gegen Ihren Heuschnupfen?
   Are you taking anything __________ your hay fever?
3. Wir müssten irgendwann gegen 10 Uhr ankommen.
   We should arrive sometime __________ 10 o'clock.
4. Die Mannschaft hat gegen eine viel schwächere verloren.
   The team lost __________ a much weaker one.
5. Es hat viel Widerstand gegen den Plan gegeben.
   There has been a lot of resistance __________ the plan.
6. Er war zu schnell und ist gegen eine Mauer gefahren.
   He was too fast and drove __________ a wall.
7. Die Geiseln wurden gegen Gefangene ausgetauscht.
   The hostages were exchanged __________ prisoners.

211 A play *spielen*

Wählen Sie die richtige Lösung, a oder b.

I can't (a.) act / (b.) play theatre (1.), but I enjoy going to the theatre. Our local theatre recently (a.) performed / (b.) played (2.) a comedy that (a.) was set / (b.) played (3.) in the 1980s. Somebody I know (a.) acted / (b.) played (4.) the lead. He (a.) acted / (b.) played (5.) a footballer who loves scoring own goals.

1	2	3	4	5

212 Big, tall, great? *groß*

Ergänzen Sie.

big • great • large • tall

1. Jem's over 1 metre 90 ____________.
2. Will it make a ____________ difference?
3. I have ____________ respect for her.
4. It was a ____________ mistake to invite Adrian.
5. They paid a very ____________ amount.
6. Personal coaching is ____________ business these days.
7. Was Obama a ____________ president?
8. Fiona is my ____________ sister. She's two years older.
9. It was a moment of ____________ danger.
10. Who lives in that ____________ house at the end of the road?
11. She's almost forgotten now, but 20 years ago she was a ____________ star.
12. He was a good teacher. He had ____________ patience[1] and understanding.

[1] Geduld

213 Small or little? *klein*

Ergänzen Sie *small* oder *little*.

1. Which number is ___________er: 2.75 or 2?
2. She's just given birth to a ___________ boy.
3. They live in a lovely ___________ village on the lakeside.
4. The password is 'admin', all in ___________ letters.
5. You only need a ___________ amount of sugar.
6. Do you have any ___________ change, for the parking meter[1]?
7. The room was a bit ___________, but it was OK for one night.
8. A ___________ car uses less petrol.
9. Our ex-boss was a nasty ___________ man.
10. Joey is my ___________ brother. I'm a year older than him.

214 What was that? *verstehen*

Was ist richtig: a oder b?

1. Could you speak a bit louder, please. At the back of the room here we can't (a.) hear / (b.) understand what you're saying.
2. The article was about molecules and atomic particles. I'm not a scientist[2] and I couldn't (a.) hear / (b.) understand what it was all about.
3. Can you hold on a minute while I just shut my door. That group of visitors is making so much noise that I can't (a.) hear / (b.) understand you properly.

1	2	3

[1] Parkuhr
[2] Wissenschaftler/in

215 A crossword *bleiben*

Ergänzen Sie.

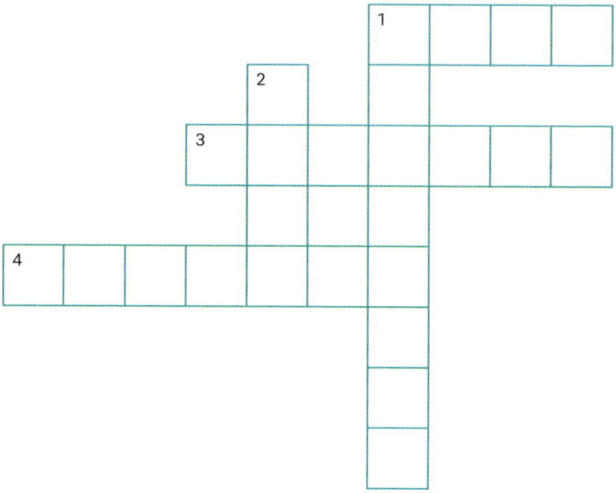

Across

1. How long do you want to _ _ _ _? One night or two?
3. Little _ _ _ _ _ _ _ to be done. Most things are now under control.
4. What's the time? This clock seems to have _ _ _ _ _ _ _.

Down

1. We all remained _ _ _ _ _ _ _ _ until the guest of honour sat down.
2. Please _ _ _ _ quiet, or you'll frighten it away.

216 A question of speed *schnell*

Ergänzen Sie *fast* oder *quick(ly)*.

1. The car wasn't driving very ____________ .
2. I'll just have a ____________ look at the latest news.
3. It's a good ____________ road with little traffic.
4. We've got time for a ____________ cup of coffee.
5. Wilson ran one of the ____________*est* races of her career.
6. Can you tell me ____________ what I'll need to take with me?

217 Places *Platz*

Welcher Ausdruck ist richtig?

1. Can you make ... for one more?
   - place
   - room

2. In the centre of town there is a big ... .
   - place
   - square

3. ◆ Excuse me, ...?
   ● Sorry. Someone's sitting there.
   - is this place free
   - is this seat taken

4. The hotel has two tennis ... .
   - courts
   - places
   - pitches

5. It also has a golf ... .
   - course
   - court
   - place

6. The school sold its ... for redevelopment, to raise money.
   - sport field
   - sport place
   - sports ground

7. Janice has got a ... at one of the elite universities.
   - place
   - study place
   - studying place

8. Come in and ... .
   - have a seat
   - take place

9. Down by the river would be a good ... to have our barbecue party.
   - place
   - space

10. There's ... for the rest of the books in this box here.
    - place
    - room

218 Getting from A to B *Reise, Fahrt*

Was passt in die Lücke? Mehrere Lösungen sind möglich.

1. ◆ We weren't expecting you this early.
   ● Yes, it was a very easy ... today, there was very little traffic on the road.
   ◯ drive ◯ journey ◯ trip

2. ◆ Do you think you could look after our dog one weekend?
   ● Sure. You want to go away?
   ◆ Yes, we'd like to go on a ... to Amsterdam.
   ◯ weekend travel ◯ weekend trip ◯ weekend journey

3. ● How far are you from the centre of town?
   ◆ Just a ... .
   ◯ ten-minute bus ride ◯ journey of ten minutes with the bus ◯ short drive by bus

4. ◆ Would you describe ... as one of your hobbies?
   ● It would be if I could afford to get away more often!
   ◯ travels ◯ travel ◯ journeying

5. ◆ Have you been to Bulgaria before?
   ● No. We've booked a ten-day guided ... so that we can get a feel for the country.
   ◯ journey ◯ trip ◯ tour

6. ◆ We need to cut down on our outgoings[1].
   ● Well, one way would be to reduce the number of ... we make.
   ◯ car travels ◯ car drives ◯ car journeys

[1] Ausgaben

219 How long? *brauchen*

Drücken Sie den Sachverhalt besser aus – benutzen Sie *take*.

◆ How long ~~do I need~~ from here to Strasbourg?

1. ______________________________

● ~~You need~~ about four hours by car.

2. ______________________________

◆ ~~I needed~~ two whole days to get my presentation ready.

3. ______________________________

● I know. That sort of thing ~~needs~~ a lot of time.

4. ______________________________

220 This takes an hour *dauern, brauchen*

Übersetzen Sie.

1. Ich brauche deine Hilfe. Es dauert nur ein paar Minuten.

____

2. Du brauchst nicht auf mich zu warten.

____

3. Mit dem Zug braucht man anderthalb Stunden.

____

4. Die Reise dauert anderthalb Stunden.

____

5. Der Film dauert 30 Minuten.

____

6. Sie brauchen nichts mitzubringen, wir haben alles.

____

7. Ich brauche noch zwei Stunden. Für diese Art von Arbeit braucht man lange.

____

221 Will it hold? *halten*

Was ist richtig: a oder b?

1. Will the fine weather (a.) keep / (b.) hold till the weekend?
2. (a.) Hold / (b.) Stop the thief!
3. The crisis (a.) held on / (b.) lasted for well over a year.
4. What's that (a.) you're holding / (b.) you're keeping in your hand? Can I see?
5. We always (a.) held him for trustworthy[1] / (b.) thought of him as trustworthy.
6. I was so tired, I could hardly (a.) hold / (b.) keep my eyes open.
7. The eggs will (a.) hold / (b.) keep longer in the fridge of course.
8. I need some light. Can you (a.) hold / (b.) keep the torch for me while I try and see what's wrong?
9. Which driver (a.) holds / (b.) keeps the record for the Monza circuit?
10. If you want to be trusted, you have to (a.) hold to / (b.) stick to the rules.
11. I don't trust them. They never (a.) hold / (b.) keep their promise.
12. Just (a.) hold to / (b.) keep to the left and you'll be OK.
13. I mustn't (a.) hold you / (b.) keep you. I expect you have lots to do.
14. To mark the occasion[2], the vice-president (a.) held / (b.) made a short speech.
15. The friendship didn't (a.) hold / (b.) last long.
16. Can you (a.) hold / (b.) keep your breath for a minute? Try it.

1	2	3	4	5	6	7	8

9	10	11	12	13	14	15	16

[1] vertrauenswürdig
[2] Zur Feier des Tages

222 How about Wednesday? *passen*

Ergänzen Sie.

fit • match • suit

1. How about Wednesday? Does that __________ you?
2. I always used to think that green didn't __________ me.
3. If the text doesn't __________, you can take this paragraph out.
4. This chair is not quite so wide and should ________ in the corner quite nicely.
5. You can't wear that jacket with those trousers. They don't __________.

223 What's your son doing? *Studium, studieren*

Was passt in die Lücke? Mehrere Lösungen sind möglich.

1. What's your son doing now? – He ...
   a. is a student c. is at university
   b. studies economics d. studies
2. A lot of top managers in fact never ...
   a. studyed c. were on the university
   b. did a study d. went to university
3. A lot of ... in Britain last not more than three years.
   a. courses c. degree courses
   b. studies d. university courses
4. When are you going to ... ?
   a. begin your study c. start university
   b. begin the studies d. start the university
5. What ... has she chosen?
   a. course c. study
   b. subject d. study course

1	2	3	4	5

18

224 By or not by? *bei*

Korrigieren Sie.

1. We didn't stay in a hotel. We stayed ~~by~~ __________ friends.
2. I'm staying ~~by~~ __________ Leonard's place. He has a spare room.
3. ~~By~~ __________ so many problems, it's difficult to know where to start.
4. We live ~~by~~ __________ Hamburg.
5. I work ~~by~~ __________ a firm in the textile industry.
6. She met her partner ~~by~~ __________ a seminar.
7. Let's discuss this in peace and quiet ~~by~~ __________ a glass of wine.
8. People say the view is best ~~by~~ __________ sunset.
9. He died ~~by~~ __________ a car accident.
10. I'm afraid I only have €20 ~~by~~ __________ me.
11. Guess who I met ~~by~~ __________ the baker's this morning.
12. I stood and watched her ~~by~~ __________ her work.
13. It was not very comfortable ~~by~~ __________ the temperature around zero.

225 On the job *Arbeit*

Ergänzen Sie *work* oder *job*.

- ◆ What's your (1.) ____________?
- ● I'm a photographer.
- ◆ That sounds like interesting (2.) ____________.
- ● That's what most people think, but it's actually quite hard (3.) ____________, with a lot of stress if you want to make money at it. It's certainly not my dream (4.) ____________.
- ◆ OK.
- ● I'm hoping to change my (5.) ____________. What I'd really like is a (6.) ____________ with animals.

226 A changed man *(an)erkennen*

Ergänzen Sie *realized* oder *recognized*.

1. He'd lost so much weight that I hardly ____________ him.
2. Few people ____________ how serious the problem was.
3. I suddenly ____________ that I had no money on me.
4. Nobody ____________ what had happened till it was too late.
5. Several governments have already ____________ the new regime.

227 A crossword *endlich, schließlich*

Ergänzen Sie.

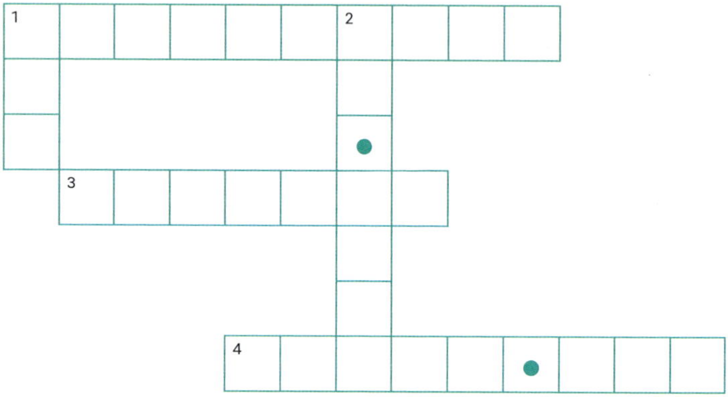

Across

1. It was a long search, but e _ _ _ _ _ _ _ _ y we found what we were looking for.
3. It's f _ _ _ _ _ y stopped raining!
4. You can't expect too much of him, a _ _ _ _ a _ _ he's still only 14.

Down

1. I made several offers to help, but he didn't respond, so in the _ _ _ I just left him to it.
2. We've paid off all our debts, a _ l _ _ _!

228 A question of weight *leicht*

Wählen Sie die richtige Lösung.

1. This bag is so … . It feels as though it's empty.
   - easy
   - light
   - slight
2. I'm afraid we seem to have a … problem.
   - easy
   - light
   - slight
3. The exam was actually quite … .
   - easy
   - light
   - slight
4. There has been … improvement in the economic situation.
   - an easy
   - a light
   - a slight
5. … wind was blowing from the northeast.
   - An easy
   - A light
   - A slight
6. There was only one really acceptable offer, so … to decide which to accept.
   - I found it easy
   - It fell easy
   - It was a slight question

229 Not from *von*

Korrigieren Sie.

1. It's one of many films ~~from~~ Steven Spielberg.

   ____

2. Oxford is northwest ~~from~~ London.

   ____

3. Six ~~from~~ ten people think the government has handled the crisis well.

   ____

4. Jason is a friend ~~from me~~ from my schooldays.

   ____

5. This magazine article is ~~from~~ someone I know.

   ____

6. The shop is in the arcade to the right ~~from~~ the station.

   ____

230 More weight *schwer*

Was passt in die Lücke? Mehrere Lösungen sind möglich.

1. How ... is your hand luggage? — a. great b. serious c. heavy
2. I'm ... disappointed. — a. deeply b. heavily c. greatly
3. It's ... to imagine what the world would be like without it. — a. heavy b. hard c. difficult
4. I'm not really ill. It's just a ... cold. — a. heavy b. great c. deep
5. You have to be ... rich to own property in Monte Carlo. — a. heavily b. violently c. stinking
6. Some of the questions were easy, but a few were really ... . — a. heavy b. serious c. difficult
7. Fortunately, they've not been ... injured. — a. heavily b. seriously c. badly
8. ... fighting continues in the area controlled by the rebels. — a. heavy b. hard c. big
9. People like that deserve to be ... punished. — a. seriously b. deeply c. severely
10. I realize now that it was a ... mistake. — a. heavy b. serious c. big
11. Old people are often ... hearing. — a. heavy in b. hard of c. heavy
12. The storm caused ... damage. — a. grave b. serious c. severe

231 Bad and worse *schlecht*

Wählen Sie die passende Übersetzung.

1. ◆ Let's see if we can find a suitable time. How about Wednesday?
   ● *Mittwoch ist schlecht.* Could we make it Thursday instead?
   a. Wednesday is bad.
   b. Wednesday is difficult.
   c. Wednesday is poor.

2. ◆ How long do you think we'll need?
   ● *Das kann ich schlecht sagen.* Two hours, three hours, something like that.
   a. I cannot say that well.
   b. I cannot really tell it.
   c. I cannot really say.

3. ◆ What shall we tell him – if he asks?
   ● *Wir können ihm schlecht sagen, dass wir ihm nicht vertrauen.*
   a. We can hardly tell him that we don't trust him.
   b. We can't well tell him that we don't trust him.
   c. We can badly say that we don't trust him.

4. ◆ It's cold in here.
   ● Yes, I'm sorry. It's this window. *Es schließt schlecht.*
   a. It shuts badly.
   b. It doesn't shut well.
   c. It doesn't shut properly.

1	2	3	4

232 Bad for business *schlecht*

Ergänzen Sie. Verwenden Sie jedes Wort nur einmal.

bad • sick • off • poor • poorly

1. Business is not just ____________, it's terrible at present.
2. Gone are the days when Chinese products were good value for money but rather ____________ quality.
3. I don't like the look or the smell of this fish. I think it's ____________.
4. ◆ What's the matter, Jack? You don't look very well.
   ● I feel ____________.
5. The meeting was ____________ attended: only six people came.

233 All & every *alle(s)*

Übersetzen Sie.

1. Alle denken das Gleiche.

   ____

2. Ich bin bereit alles [egal was] zu tun, um dir zu helfen.

   ____

3. Alle zwei oder drei Tage bekomme ich eine E-Mail.

   ____

4. Mein Motto ist: Alles oder nichts.

   ____

5. Wir brauchen alle eine Pause.

   ____

6. Alle Leute waren begeistert.

   ____

234 Dates and deadlines *bis*

Was ist richtig: a oder b?

1. I'll wait (a.) till / (b.) to six.
2. If they haven't arrived (a.) till / (b.) by then, I'll go without them.
3. You'll have the data (a.) by / (b.) until the end of the week, I promise.
4. There must have been (a.) till / (b.) up to 100 people there.
5. In the holidays they often sleep (a.) till / (b.) to at least 11.
6. (a.) By the time / (b.) Until we'd finished, it was dark.
7. I should get home (a.) till / (b.) by about 7.30, but it might be later.
8. I can count (a.) till / (b.) up to ten in Arabic.
9. Walk along here (a.) till / (b.) as far as the Imperial Hotel.
10. The artist covered the building in silver foil from top (a.) till / (b.) to bottom.

1	2	3	4	5	6	7	8	9	10
a									

235 Twins *gleich*

Ergänzen Sie Angaben (1.) zum Alter, (2.) zur Größe und (3.) zur Kleidung.

David and Peter are twins. As twins, they are of course

(1.) ______________________. But they are also

(2.) ______________________, and they often wear

(3.) ______________________.

236 A waiter's questions *fertig*

Was fragt der Kellner? Verwenden Sie einmal *ready*, einmal *finished*.

237 A question of ability *können*

Ordnen Sie zu und ergänzen Sie die rechte Spalte.

1. Ich kann kein Spanisch.
2. Du kannst es wirklich gut!
3. Das kann ja jeder.
4. Wir können gut mit einander.
5. Wie konnten Sie nur?!
6. Ich kann einfach nicht mehr.

a. You're really good __________ it.
b. We __________ __________ well together.
c. I don't __________ Spanish.
d. I just can't __________ on.
e. Anyone can _______ that!
f. How _______ you?!

1	2	3	4	5	6

238 Change *werden*

Welcher Ausdruck ist richtig? Oder sind beide richtig?

1. Bonnie says she wants to ... a journalist when she grows up.
   - be
   - become
2. I'll ... mad if I get any more email enquiries like this.
   - become
   - go
3. It's autumn, and the leaves ... yellow, brown and red.
   - are turning
   - become
4. It ... very difficult to find new markets for our products.
   - is becoming
   - is getting
5. As I ... old, there are many things I no longer take so seriously.
   - go
   - grow
6. They were forecasting rain, but the weather ... better than expected.
   - has got
   - has turned out
7. When I heard Giorgio was coming, I ... very excited.
   - got
   - went
8. My hair ... grey, and it makes me feel old.
   - is going
   - becomes

239 Oh *(be)merken, sich merken*

Ergänzen Sie. Verwenden Sie jedes Wort nur einmal.

note • notice • realize

1. I didn't ____________ you'd already arrived. The message didn't reach me.
2. Please ____________ only 8 kg of hand luggage is allowed.
3. I ____________d that there was a small crowd of people, but at the time I didn't give it much thought.

18

240 Time *Zeit*

Korrigieren Sie.

1. I haven't seen Raymond much ~~in the last time~~.

2. ~~In the first time~~, when I was new to the job, there was a lot to learn.

3. I'm going to be travelling quite a lot ~~in the next time~~.

241 Once & more *einmal*

Übersetzen Sie. Verwenden Sie die angegebenen Ausdrücke.

1. Sind Sie schon einmal in Mexiko gewesen? *(ever)*

2 Ich war schon einmal in New York. *(before)*

3. Ich würde gern einmal Irland besuchen. *(sometime)*

4. Hören Sie gut zu, denn ich sage es nur einmal. *(once)*

5. Es war einmal ein König ... *(once upon a time)*

6. Die Stadt war einmal berühmt. *(once)*

242 In the past *früher, frühere(r/s)*

Welcher Ausdruck ist richtig?

1. It's her second marriage. Her ... was called Heinz, too.
   - earlier husband
   - ex-husband
   - husband before
2. They each have a son from ... .
   - an ex-marriage
   - a previous marriage
   - a marriage before
3. We ... in Hamburg.
   - lived earlier
   - former lived
   - used to live
4. I apologize for my lateness. I couldn't make it any ... .
   - more earlier
   - more previously
   - sooner
5. It was ... a nice place to live, but all this new development has spoiled it.
   - earlier
   - once
   - sooner
6. For sale. Only one ... owner.
   - earlier
   - former
   - previous
7. I was born and grew up in the ... East Germany.
   - earlier
   - former
   - previous
8. He says he won't be able to attend 'because of ... engagement'.
   - an earlier
   - a former
   - a previous
9. The place was ... quite famous.
   - earlier
   - once
   - earlier once
10. We ... quite often.
    - used to meet
    - met earlier
    - met previously

243 A question of position *stehen*

Ergänzen Sie die Übersetzung.

1. Tut mir leid, er steht unter der Dusche.
   Sorry, ____________________ a shower.
2. In der Zeitung steht, dass Monkton gewonnen hat.
   In the paper ____________________ that Monkton has won.
3. Gelb steht dir.
   Yellow ____________________ you.
4. Der Zug war voll und ich musste stehen.
   The train was full and I had to ____________________ .
5. Der Rettungsplan steht jetzt.
   The rescue plan ____________________ .

244 While or during? *während*

Wählen Sie die richtige Lösung.

(a.) During / (b.) While (1.) students, James and I had weekend and evening jobs at the same restaurant for several months. He worked in the kitchen, (a.) during / (b.) while (2.) I served out front. We worked there (a.) during / (b.) while (3.) the summer holidays, too. It was hard, I remember, because we didn't have a single day off (a.) while / (b.) throughout the whole eight weeks (4.).

1	2	3	4

245 Power *stark*

Welcher Ausdruck passt in die Lücke?

1. There is a ... westerly wind.
   - heavy
   - powerful
   - strong

2. He was once a ... smoker.
   - strong
   - heavy
   - great

3. It's been raining ... all morning.
   - strongly
   - heavily
   - violently

4. Expect another ... frost tonight.
   - powerful
   - hard
   - strong

5. Fortunately she's not in ... pain.
   - great
   - heavy
   - strong

6. There's ... traffic on all roads out of the capital.
   - strong
   - heavy
   - hard

7. The roof has been ... damaged.
   - strongly
   - hard
   - badly

8. I'm afraid I have ... reservations[1] about the plan.
   - strong
   - grand
   - violent

9. We are ... dependent on what happens in the global economy.
   - strongly
   - heavily
   - much

10. She published her memoirs in a ... book.
    - 600-page long
    - 600-page strong
    - 600-page heavy

[1] Vorbehalte, Zweifel

246 A crossword *vor*

Ergänzen Sie.

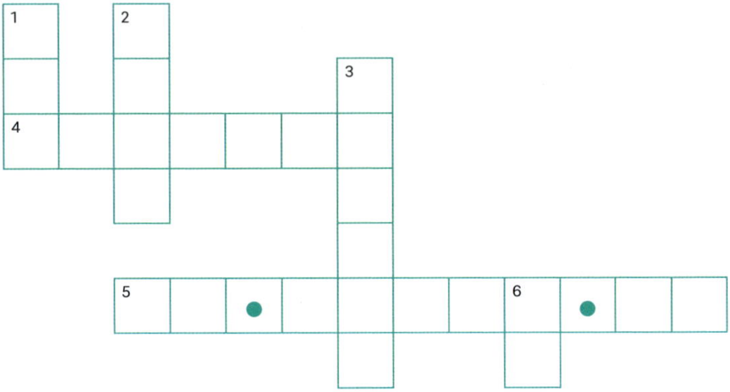

Across

4. I'll meet you o _ _ _ _ _ _ the main entrance.
5. You can't park i _ f _ _ _ _ o _ the building, only at the back.

Down

1. I spoke to him only ten minutes _ _ _.
2. He was trembling[1] w _ _ _ fear.
3. I'll try and be there b _ _ _ _ _ the others.
6. It's two minutes _ _ two.

[1] zitterte

247 Not busy *ruhig*

Ergänzen Sie.

calm • quiet • still

1. We live in a __________ street in the suburbs.
2. She always seems to have everything under control and remains __________ in the wildest chaos.
3. The wind was light, the sea was nice and __________.
4. Is something troubling you? You're so __________. You've not said anything all evening.
5. If you won't sit __________, how am I supposed to put the plaster on?

248 How? *wie*

Übersetzen Sie.

1. Wie läuft es? Alles in Ordnung?

   ____

2. Wie war das Wetter?

   ____

3. Wie ist der neue Chef?

   ____

4. Wie sagt man das auf Englisch?

   ____

5. Er ist nicht so alt wie sie.

   ____

6. Wie ist die Telefonnummer?

   ____

7. Wie war es, allein zu reisen?

   ____

8. Es ist ein Gebäude wie ein Hotel.

   ____

249 With us or against us? *auch*

Welcher Ausdruck passt in die Lücke?

1. Wallis is normally against this sort of idea, but ... he seems to be in favour.
   - also
   - even
   - too

2. ◆ I need a break.
   ● ... .
   - I also
   - Me too
   - I as well

3. ◆ I like the design.
   ● ... .
   - I also
   - So do I
   - So do I too

4. ◆ We won't arrive till quite late.
   ● ... .
   - Neither will we
   - Nor we
   - We also not

5. ◆ I'm afraid I haven't understood this.
   ● You're not the only one. I don't understand it ... .
   - too
   - either
   - nor

6. ... it costs more, I think this is the better solution.
   - Also if
   - Even if
   - Even when

7. The roof has been damaged and ... have two windows.
   - also
   - even
   - so

250 I know *bewusst*

Ergänzen Sie *aware* oder *conscious*.

1. I'm very ______________ that this is not an easy decision for you.
2. As far as I'm ______________, no other company has a comparable product.
3. I didn't ______________ly try to take advantage of the situation.
4. It was not a very ______________ decision on my part.
5. People nowadays are very energy-______________, partly because of the cost of energy, partly for environmental reasons.

251 Permission to drive *Führerschein*

Übersetzen Sie.

1. Die Polizei wollte meinen Führerschein sehen.

   ____

2. Unser Sohn hat gerade angefangen, den Führerschein zu machen.

   ____

3. Unsere Tochter hat bereits den Führerschein.

   ____

252 Having things with you *tragen*

Ergänzen Sie.

bear • carry • support • wear

1. How formal is this event? What should I ______________?
2. That looks heavy. I'll help you ______________ it.
3. The platform is ______________ed by one central pillar[1].
4. You should ______________ some sort of ID with you at all times.
5. It's a terrible responsibility for her to have to ______________ on her own.
6. Let's hope all this hard work eventually ______________s fruit.
7. I don't normally ______________ a watch at the weekend. My life is so governed by the clock during the week.
8. Who is going to ______________ the costs – us or them?
9. Didn't you use to ______________ glasses?

[1] Säule

253 Up there *über*

Was passt in die Lücke? Mehrere Lösungen sind möglich.

1. Jackson's office is on the floor ... us. — a. above b. over
2. Andy was in the class ... me at school. — a. above b. over
3. She's always complaining ... the food. — a. about b. on c. over
4. I'm travelling ... Frankfurt because the flight's cheaper. — a. by the way of b. over c. via
5. It can only be a few degrees ... freezing this morning. — a. above b. over c. up of
6. Results this year were well ... average. — a. above b. beyond c. over
7. It took her two years to get ... his death. — a. above b. beyond c. over
8. He's the sort of person who laughs ... his own jokes. — a. above b. at c. over
9. The city is about 600 metres ... sea level. — a. above b. beyond c. over
10. Tears ran ... his face. — a. about b. down c. over
11. Is there any money ...? — a. left b. over c. resting
12. We'll be at home ... Christmas this year. — a. at b. during c. over
13. There's no reason to get annoyed ... it. — a. above b. about c. over
14. Her books are famous ... the borders of Wyoming. — a. above b. beyond c. over
15. They sent a bill ... €60,000. — a. over above b. for over c. over more than

254 Already and more *schon*

Muss der Ausdruck mit „schon" übersetzt werden – ja oder nein?

1. Es ist *schon* ganz schön schwierig sich zu entscheiden.
2. Wir haben *schon* halb drei.
3. Was macht es *schon* für einen Unterschied?
4. Hat Tony *schon* angerufen?
5. *Schon* bevor er aufstand, wusste ich, was er sagen würde.
6. Ich sehe *schon*, dass wir mehr Zeit benötigen.
7. Sind Sie *schon mal* in Disneyland gewesen?
8. Die ersten Gäste sind *schon* da.
9. Was weiß er mit 18 *schon* vom Leben?
10. *Schon* bald werden wir die ersten Ergebnisse wissen.

Übersetzen Sie die Sätze, in denen „schon" mit übersetzt werden muss.

19. Confusing friends

Englische Wortpaare mit ähnlicher Form
aber unterschiedlicher Bedeutung

255 advice / advise

Ergänzen Sie.

- ◆ Do you have a moment?
- ● Sure.
- ◆ I'd like to ask your (1.) ______________.
- ● What about?
- ◆ Well, can you (2.) ______________ me what to do in a case like this? You see, ...

256 homework / housework

Ordnen Sie zu.

1. Exercises and tasks given by a teacher	a. housework
2. Cleaning, cooking, etc.	b. homework

257 interesting / interested

Wählen Sie die richtige Lösung.

- ◆ There's a photo exhibition next week about the Sahara. Are you (a.) interested / (b.) interesting (1.)? Would you like to go?
- ● It certainly sounds (a.) interested / (b.) interesting (2.). I've always (a.) been interested in / (b.) been interested for (3.) Africa.

1	2	3

258 desert / dessert

Übersetzen Sie.

1. Ist die Sahara die größte Wüste der Erde?

   ____

2. Was möchten Sie als Nachspeise?

   ____

259 economic / economical

Ergänzen Sie.

1. The ______________ situation is improving.
2. The government's ______________ policies have been successful.
3. The new models are much more ______________ and use an average of 15% less energy.
4. It's not a good idea to start a new business in the present ______________ climate.
5. It's much more ______________ to buy in bulk[1].
6. It's a brilliant design, so ______________ on space.

[1] in großen Mengen kaufen

260 classic / classical

Korrigieren Sie – falls nötig!

1. I don't listen to much *classic* ______________ music.
2. This is a *classic* ______________ case of poor communication.
3. I can't understand people who go to university to study *classic* ______________ Greek.
4. Spielberg has directed a number of *classic* ______________ films.
5. I made the *classic* ______________ mistake.
6. She's just as much at home in *classic* ______________ theatre as in contemporary plays.

19

261 beside / besides

Welcher Ausdruck ist richtig?

1. Come and sit ... me.
   - beside
   - besides
2. Do you know anyone else ... the hosts?
   - beside
   - besides
3. I don't have time, and ..., it costs too much.
   - beside
   - besides
4. I do several other sports ... sailing.
   - beside
   - besides
5. ... full time, I also perform as a cabaret artist.
   - Besides to work
   - Besides working
6. My problems seem so insignificant ... yours.
   - beside
   - besides

262 it's / its

Ergänzen Sie.

1. ____________ so cold in here!
2. The car has some rust, but ____________ engine is OK.
3. The hospital has ____________ own emergency power supply.
4. Somehow the company seems to have lost ____________ way.
5. ____________ called *The Arena*.
6. Sorry, what's ____________ name?

263 all together / altogether

Ergänzen Sie.

1. ◆ Are you paying separately or together?
   ● Well, how much is it ______________?
   ◆ €146.80.
   ● OK, together.

2. ◆ It seems ages since we last met.
   ● It is, in fact I can't remember the last time we were
   ____

264 lay / lie

Ergänzen Sie die passende Verbform.

1. Jacob's tired. He's just gone to ______________ down for a bit.
2. I hate it when Mr Smithers ______________ his hand on my arm.
3. Just think. All this stuff has ______________ here unnoticed for over 50 years.
4. I'm sorry. I ______________ to you, but it was because I wanted to protect you from the truth.
5. This time last week we were ______________ on the beach with not a care in the world.
6. The new carpets are being ______________ today.
7. What's that ______________ on the floor? It looks like a banknote.
8. Snow ______________ on the ground and it was bitterly cold.

	Infinitiv	*Vergangenheit*	*Present Perfect*
9.	(to) lay (*legen*)	______________	have/has ______________
10.	(to) lie (*liegen*)	______________	have/has ______________
11.	(to) lie (*lügen*)	______________	have/has ______________

265 greatly / largely

Kreuzen Sie die richtige Lösung an.

	greatly	largely	
1.	○	○	The forest fires are now ... under control.
2.	○	○	Success is ... a question of who you know.
3.	○	○	Reactions have varied ... .
4.	○	○	Any help would be ... appreciated.

266 past / passed

Ergänzen Sie.

1. We're on the M3 and have just ______________ exit 12, so we should be with you in about another 20 minutes.
2. We've driven ______________ exit 12.
3. Half an hour ______________ without anything new happening.
4. Has anything happened in the ______________ half hour?
5. It's now ten ______________ four.
6. I thought I just heard someone walk ______________ my door.
7. In the ______________ this place was actually quite famous.
8. But those days have ______________.

267 terrible / terrific

Ordnen Sie zu.

1. We've had a terrific holiday.	a. It's been absolutely fabulous.
2. We've had a terrible holiday.	b. Everything that could go wrong did go wrong.

268 used to / be/get used to

Welcher Ausdruck passt in die Lücke?

1. I ... for an Italian company before I came here.
   - used to work
   - am used to work
   - get used to working

2. When I broke my arm, I suddenly ... with my left hand.
   - used to write
   - was used to write
   - had to get used to writing

3. It comes as a shock to most people, but you ... after a while.
   - use to it
   - are used it
   - get used to it

4. I ... English in my job. It comes naturally now.
   - used to use
   - am used to using
   - am used to use

269 at last / at least

Ergänzen Sie.

- The documentation is complete (1.) ________________.
- How long has it taken to produce it?
- I can't remember when we started, but it must be (2.) ________________ six months ago.

270 raise / rise

Ergänzen Sie die passende Verbform.

1. The price of petrol has ________________ again.
2. They've ________________ prices again.
3. I ________________ my arm to signal that I had a question.
4. Tension ________________ in the room as the discussion intensified.
5. It was mid-winter and the sun ________________ late.
6. We need to ________________ standards.

19

271 sometime / sometimes

Was ist richtig: a oder b?

- I hope we meet again (a.) sometime / (b.) sometimes (1.).
- Yes, that would be nice.
- I (a.) sometime / (b.) sometimes (2.) have to go to Antwerp on business. Maybe we could meet up there?

272 everyday / every day

Wählen Sie die richtige Lösung.

- This sort of thing doesn't happen (a.) every day / (b.) everyday (1.) thank goodness!
- Absolutely! Can you imagine what would happen if this was an (a.) every day / (b.) everyday (2.) occurrence?

273 historic / historical

Kreuzen Sie die richtige Lösung an.

	historic	historical	
1.	○	○	It was a ... day when peace was declared.
2.	○	○	What you've just told me – is it myth or ... fact?
3.	○	○	People in ... costumes act as guides round the museum.
4.	○	○	Can you explain the ... background to the conflict?

274 affect / effect

Wählen Sie die richtige Lösung.

- What (a.) affect / (b.) effect (1.) are all these changes going to have on us personally, in this department?
- To be honest, I don't think they're going to (a.) affect / (b.) effect (2.) us much at all.

275 loose / lose

Ergänzen Sie.

1. There was a ______________ connection in the plug, that's why the hair dryer wasn't working.
2. Don't ______________ the key, or we shall be in real trouble!
3. Please don't go. It's dangerous and I don't want to ______________ you.
4. It's often cheaper to buy things ______________ rather than packaged.

276 major / mayor

Wer ist was?

1. ______________________________ 2. ______________________________

277 in time / on time

Was ist richtig: a oder b?

1. We arrived dead (a.) in / (b.) on time.
2. The train is almost always late, but today, for once, it was (a.) in / (b.) on time.
3. I hope to get there (a.) in / (b.) on time to see the end of the match.

20. All friends together

Gemischte Übungen

278 In the pub

Korrigieren Sie.

1. I ~~become~~ a Guinness, please.
2. I'd like something to eat, too. Can I see the ~~card~~, please?
3. People say English ~~kitchen~~ is not very good, but I don't believe that.
4. Oh, excuse me. My ~~handy~~ is ringing.
5. This is a really nice old ~~guesthouse~~. I come here most days on my way home from work.
6. This smoking ban – do you agree with it? What's your ~~meaning~~?

279 An evening at the theatre

Ergänzen Sie. Wählen Sie aus der folgenden Auswahl.

audience • badly visited • interval • pause
piece • play • poorly attended • public spectator

◆ So how was it? Did you enjoy the (1.) ______________?

● Yes, I did. But it was only a very small (2.) ______________.
And quite a few of those who were there left in the (3.) ______________.

◆ I should have come with you. I hate it when the performances are so (4.) ______________.

280 Television

Korrigieren Sie.

It's difficult to imagine the days when there was no (1.) ~~private~~ ____________ ____________ television and there were only two or three state-financed TV (2.) ~~programmes~~ ____________ to choose from. Those were the days when (3.) ~~newsspeakers~~ ____________ never smiled, but read the (4.) ~~newest~~ ____________ news as if they were at a funeral!

281 Changes at work

Was ist richtig: a oder b?

- ◆ How long have you been working here?
- ● (1.) (a.) For / (b.) Since almost ten years. And you?
- ◆ Only (2.) (a.) for / (b.) since the beginning of the year.
- ● There have been a lot of changes here (3.) (a.) in the last time / (b.) recently, with a lot of restructuring. It's been the same throughout the banking (4.) (a.) branch / (b.) business. The (5.) (a.) economic / (b.) economical climate is quite different from (6.) (a.) a few years ago / (b.) before a few years.

282 In the canteen

Übersetzen Sie.

- ◆ Excuse me, there aren't any (1.) *Tabletts* ____________.
- ● Some more are just coming.
- ◆ Thanks. And what's on the (2.) *Speiseplan* ____________ today?
- ● Vegetarian quiche, or chicken, or you can help yourself from the (3.) *Salatbar* ____________.
- ◆ I'll do that. Salad is (4.) *gesund* ____________.

  …

  Oh, excuse me. Where's the (5.) *Salatsoße* ____________?

283 Telephoning

Welcher Ausdruck passt in die Lücke?

1. The phone's ringing. If I ... I'll miss my bus. Can you do it, please?
   - answer it
   - go on it
2. What's the ... for France? Is it 0033?
   - pre-number
   - code
3. Do you want to ..., or shall I say you're not here?
   - accept the conversation
   - take the call
4. When you call back, ... Jane Summertown, then you'll be connected straight to me.
   - ask for
   - demand
5. What number do I have to ... for the police in this country?
   - choose
   - dial
6. The line went dead so I ... .
   - hung up
   - laid the phone down

284 At school

Korrigieren Sie.

I've just had an invitation to a class ~~meeting~~ ______________ (1.) at my old school, but I don't think I'm going to go. It was a ~~gymnasium~~ ______________ (2.) where all the doctors and lawyers and professional people sent their kids. I never felt that I belonged. I was good ~~in~~ ______________ (3.) most subjects, and I got good ~~notes~~ ______________ (4.) when we ~~wrote~~ ______________ (5.) tests, but I was never ""really happy there. I wasn't ~~mobbed~~ ______________ (6.) or anything like that, but I was certainly glad when I ~~made~~ ______________ (7.) my final exam, left and ~~started my study~~ ______________ (8.).

285 Back from holiday

Ergänzen Sie die Übersetzung.

1. Wir haben eine Rundreise durch das ganze Land gemacht.
   We _______________ a tour through the whole country.

2. Wir haben nicht in Hotels gewohnt.
   We didn't _______________ in hotels.

3. Wir haben in einfachen Pensionen übernachtet.
   We overnighted in simple _______________.

4. In Zimmern mit Warm- und Kaltwasser.
   In rooms with _______________ and cold water.

5. Die Reise dorthin hat lange gedauert.
   The journey there _______________ a long time.

6. Wir haben lange gebraucht.
   _________ _________ _________ a long time.

7. Unsere Pässe wurden ziemlich oft kontrolliert.
   Our passports were _______________ quite often.

8. Und wir mussten ständig Formulare ausfüllen.
   And we constantly had to fill in _______________.

9. Insgesamt war es eine tolle Reise.
   _______________ it was a great trip.

286 At the weekend

Welcher Ausdruck ist richtig?

1. A lot of people like to ... at the weekend, but that's not my thing.
   - sleep in
   - sleep out
2. Often I go out for a ... on my motorbike.
   - drive
   - ride
3. I ... a car.
   - used to drive
   - used to driving
4. But ... I sold the car and bought this motorbike.
   - before two years
   - two years ago
5. I ... my driving test for it a couple of months later.
   - made
   - took
6. The test wasn't very ... .
   - hard
   - heavy
7. But I'm not on the ... all the time.
   - road
   - street
8. I also like to be out and about, in ... .
   - the free nature
   - the open air
9. I quite often go ... in the mountains, especially in the autumn.
   - hiking
   - wandering
10. Usually with my camera, because I'm a bit of an amateur ... .
    - photograph
    - photographer
11. I ... the cinema.
    - am also interested in
    - also have interest for
12. You name any ... Hollywood film, I've seen it.
    - classic
    - classical
13. My favourites are ones that ... the first half of the 20th century.
    - are set in
    - play in

287 Expressions of time

Korrigieren Sie.

Meeting an old friend

- You're looking a bit tired.
- Well, I've been under quite a lot of stress (1.) ~~in the last time~~ ______________. You see, I started a new job (2.) ~~a quarter year~~ ______________ ago.

In the office

- What's the (3.) ~~newest~~ ______________ news on the joint venture in China?
- (4.) ~~In this stadium~~ ______________ of the project a lot of things are still unclear.

On the radio

- It's three minutes past eleven, and here's Steve Mapleton with up-to-date news and information on the (5.) ~~actual~~ ______________ traffic situation.

In a meeting

- I suggest we discuss this later, perhaps (6.) ~~while~~ ______________ lunch.
- Yes, it's going to (7.) ~~cost~~ ______________ too much time to do it now.

At tourist information

- There's a shuttle bus, or you can walk.
- How long (8.) ~~do you need~~ ______________ to walk?
- Not more (9.) ~~as~~ ______________ fifteen mintes.

288 People

Übersetzen Sie.

1. Ronaldos Frau ist mir sehr sympathisch.

2. Anna ist sehr selbstbewusst.

3. Mark ist mein Sohn aus früherer Ehe.

4. Ich bin gleich alt wie mein Chef.

5. Sei vorsichtig. Er ist sehr sensibel.

6. Bitte lass mich in Ruhe! Ich muss arbeiten.

7. Mein Reitlehrer ist sehr groß, fast zwei Meter groß.

8. Sei vernünftig!

9. Warum sind Sie heute so ruhig?

10. Wann waren wir das letzte Mal alle zusammen?

11. Mein Mann ist einer der wenigen Männer, die sich nicht für Fußball interessieren.

12. Die Kinder waren ganz brav.

289 A question of health

Welcher Ausdruck ist richtig?

1. Thank you for calling the Exbridge Health Centre. ... are Monday to Friday, 9 to 12.30, and 3 to 6.30.
   - Consult times
   - Speaking times
   - Surgery hours
2. They say fruit and vegetables are ..., but only of course if they aren't full of pesticides and things.
   - good for you
   - healthy for you
   - good for health
3. The doctor gave me a ... for some pills.
   - recipe
   - prescription
   - receipt
4. They gave me some ... for the first few days after the operation.
   - pain medicine
   - pain tablets
   - painkillers
5. Grandpa can't find his ... .
   - false teeth
   - replacement teeth
   - third teeth
6. You're going to have to take over the presentation. I have ..., I can hardly speak.
   - a really bad sore throat
   - really strong throat pains
   - really bad throat pains

290 Tricky pairs

Ergänzen Sie.

nearest, next

1. The train is now approaching Aldringham. Aldringham is the ______________ station stop.
2. Where's the ______________ station to the hotel?

shade, shadow

3. It's too hot in the sun for me, I'm going to have to move into the ______________.
4. I thought I saw a ______________ on the wall.

back, backside

5. For goodness sake, get up off your ______________ and do some work!
6. There are parking spaces at the ______________ of the building.

291 Food & drink

Korrigieren Sie.

1. You can't grow much on a balcony this size, just a few tomatoes, herbs and a couple of ~~salad~~ ______________ plants.
2. The fish is served with ~~salt potatoes~~ ______________ and a green salad.
3. This curry is ~~sharp~~ ______________! How much chili powder did you put in it?
4. The quality of our ~~drink water~~ ______________ is actually very good.
5. I need a ~~tablet~~ ______________ to carry all these glasses.
6. ~~Good appetite~~ ______________ everyone!
7. I'm trying to lose weight and cut down on any food that ~~makes fat~~ ______________.
8. We're planning to ~~grill~~ ______________ this evening in the back yard. Why don't you join us?
9. I think it's true that you feel better if you have one ~~warm~~ ______________ meal a day.
10. What shall I do with the ~~rests~~ ______________ from lunch? Feed them to the dog?
11. We don't eat much bread. If we buy a big ~~bread~~ ______________ we often end up throwing half of it away because it's gone stale.
12. Ann has emailed the ~~receipt~~ ______________ for that Moroccan dish she served last weekend.
13. You could have put a bit less vinegar in the salad ~~sauce~~ ______________. It's a bit sour.
14. What's on the ~~card~~ ______________ today? – It's Friday, so it's fish!
15. A lunch ~~pause~~ ______________, what's that? I never have time.
16. We stopped at this ~~guesthouse~~ ______________ called *Zum weißen Lamm* and had a fantastic German meal.

20

292 At work

Übersetzen Sie die deutschen Wörter und ergänzen Sie den Text.

My company has just been taken over, but most of the *(Personal)* 1. ________________ have kept their jobs. A couple of the older ones *(sind in Rente gegangen)* 2. ________________________________.
Business is good and a lot of us *(machen Überstunden)* 3. ________________________ on a regular basis. Our new (*Chef*) 4. ________________, or rather the new owner of the company, is an *(Unternehmer)* 5. ________________ with business interests worldwide. He only *(trifft)* 6. ________________ the big decisions and leaves the day-to-day running of his companies to local managers.

293 Business matters

Welcher Ausdruck passt in die Lücke?

1. The … risk on this project is great, but so too are the rewards.
   a. economic b. economical c. economous
2. Our bank account looks healthy, we are … .
   a. in plus b. in the red c. in the black
3. We must prevent this happening … .
   a. at every price b. on any price c. at all costs
4. It's a non-profit organization. They … any surplus they make to charity.
   a. donate b. spend c. transfer
5. Who is going to … all the extra research?
   a. pay b. pay for c. balance
6. I don't like … financial risks.
   a. going into b. making c. taking

1	2	3	4	5	6

Lösungen

1. Einfache Form und Verlaufsform

1 2. h 3. d 4. c 5. b 6. a 7. e 8. f

2 1. b 2. a 3. a, c 4. b, d 5. a 6. b, c

> ▶ **Verlaufsform (mit -ing):**
> eine gerade ablaufende Tätigkeit, eine vorübergehende Situation, eine noch nicht abgeschlossene Entwicklung.
> **Einfache Form:** Dauerzustand oder Gewohnheit.
> Verben, die einen Zustand, d.h. keine Tätigkeit ausdrücken, können nicht in der Verlaufsform stehen.

3 2. I don't think so. 3. It's snowing 4. is shining 5. seem 6. I can see 7. is just arriving

4 2. I'm having 3. I'm having 4. I'm having 5. I'm having 6. I have 7. I have

> ▶ ***have*** drückt Tätigkeit aus: kann in der Verlaufsform stehen.
> ***have*** drückt Zustand aus: kann nur in der einfachen Form stehen.

5 2. What does this symbol mean?
3. Joanna is trying to lose some weight.
4. She doesn't eat meat.
5. The tourist office is just closing.
6. It closes earlier in the winter.
7. The situation is getting better slowly.
8. I don't remember anything.

6 2. don't know 3. aren't speaking 4. is making 5. need 6. doesn't cost 7. don't mind 8. are you doing? am trying 9. is living 10. are rising 11. are you waiting 12. does this word mean

7 2. are becoming 3. is rising 4. are taking 5. are worrying 6. are giving 7. are buying 8. are living

> ▶ Noch nicht abgeschlossene Entwicklungen: Verlaufsform

8 2. Do you remember 3. owns 4. doesn't belong 5. don't see 6. Did you understand

> ▶ Verben, die einen Zustand ausdrücken: keine Verlaufsform

9 2. korrekt 3. were still sitting 4. korrekt 5. was listening; korrekt; korrekt 6. korrekt; were discussing 7. was raining; korrekt 8. was still having; korrekt

10 2. It all depends (on) what it costs.
3. I'm working from home at the moment.
4. I'm learning Spanish.
5. When I arrived, over 50 people were (already) waiting. 6. They are building a new hotel. 7. Normally I get up / I normally get up later on Saturdays.
8. But I'm working today.

2. Present Perfect und Vergangenheit

11 2. d 3. a 4. g 5. e 6. h 7. c 8. b

12 2. b 3. a 4. b 5. b 6. a 7. a 8. b

> ▶ begin, began, begun; feel, felt, felt; fall, fell, fallen; fly, flew, flown; forget, forgot, forgotten; spend, spent, spent; swim, swam, swum; lay, laid, laid (*legen, decken*); lie, lay, lain (*liegen*)

13 Richtig: 2. a 3. a 4. b 5. b 6. a 7. a

▶ Bericht über ein in der Vergangenheit abgeschlossenes Geschehen (oft mit Zeitbestimmung der Vergangenheit): nur einfache Vergangenheit möglich.
Present Perfect: Etwas hat sich irgendwann in der Vergangenheit ereignet, der genaue Zeitpunkt ist unbekannt oder unwichtig; wichtig ist das jetzige Ergebnis.
Vergangenheitsform: Etwas geschah zu einem bestimmten Zeitpunkt. – Present Perfect: Wichtig ist allein die Tatsache, dass sich etwas ereignet hat.

14 2. I did it 3. We began 4. I spoke 5. I slept 6. He showed them round 7. I rang it/them 8. I paid it 9. Someone/They stole it

15 2. had 3. was 4. tasted 5. didn't 6. didn't 7. said 8. thought 9. have eaten 10. decided

16 2. brought 3. didn't you open *[damals, als es gekommen ist]* / haven't you opened *[es ist jetzt nicht geöffnet]* 4. haven't ordered *[es liegt keine Bestellung vor]* / didn't order *[gab keine Bestellung auf]* 5. did 6. have forgotten *[du weißt es jetzt nicht mehr]* / forgot *[nachdem du es tatest]* 7. have been 8. haven't become

▶ Bisweilen sind zwei Sichtweisen auf ein Geschehen möglich – als Ereignis zu einem bestimmten Zeitpunkt in der Vergangenheit (einfache Vergangenheitsform), oder als Ereignis irgendwann in der Vergangenheit mit einem jetzigen Ergebnis (Present Perfect).

17 2. am 3. have decided *[jetziges Ergebnis]* / decided *[Entschluss zu einem bestimmten Zeitpunkt]* 4. think 5. have had *[in der ganzen Zeit bis jetzt]* 6. broke out 7. have always looked for *[in der ganzen Zeit bis jetzt]* 8. serve / have served / served 9. have again found *[jetziges Ergebnis]*

18 2. I've checked 3. I've read 4. I've given 5. I've been 6. I've bought 7. (I've) eaten 8. I've given up

19 2. Have you ever driven 3. Have you ever drunk 4. Have you ever ridden 5. Have you ever bought 6. Have you ever worn 7. Have you ever sung 8. Have you ever eaten

20 2. was 3. have visited 4. have always loved 5. was 6. were 7. was 8. wanted 9. have often dreamt/dreamed 10. have never had 11. found 12. didn't think 13. took 14. spoke 15. had to 16. explained 17. interpreted 18. said 19. didn't understand 20. told 21. didn't want 22. has never happened

3. Present Perfect mit *since, for* und *how long*

21 2. for 3. since 4. for 5. since 6. since 7. for 8. since 9. for 10. since 11. for 12. for

22 1. a 2. b 3. a 4. a

▶ Zum Ausdruck eines Zustandes, der in der Vergangenheit begonnen hat und bis jetzt andauert, verwendet das Englische das Present Perfect, NICHT eine Gegenwartsform, oft zusammen mit *since* (+ Anfangszeitpunkt) und *for* (+ Zeitspanne) bzw. in Fragen mit *how long*.

23 2. has been, for 3. have you known 4. has been developing for 5. have calmed down, left 6. has been, for 7. has this problem existed 8. have you been

24 2. How long have you been working
3. How long have you been driving
4. How long have you been learning
5. How long have you been waiting
6. How long have you been trying
7. How long have you been sitting
8. How long have you been training
9. How long have you been planning

▶ Mit der Verlaufsform des Present Perfect wird das ununterbrochene Andauern eines Vorgangs betont.

4. Verneinung mit und ohne *do*

25 2. e 3. a 4. f 5. d 6. b 7. c

26 1. a 2. b 3. a 4. b

27 2. don't know 3. didn't walk 4. don't have 5. haven't made 6. can't speak 7. won't give 8. don't do

28 2. won't 3. didn't 4. don't 5. can't 6. haven't

29 2. It doesn't rain often / often rain. 3. We don't have ... 4. You don't have to have ... 5. korrekt

30 2. This hasn't ever happened before. 3. I didn't do this. 4. Why isn't Frank coming? 5. We didn't decide till yesterday. 6. Why don't you do more preparation? 7. I absolutely don't agree. 8. The train doesn't stop in Torquay.

31 1. I don't like this room.
2. We don't know what('s) happened.
3. He doesn't do any sport.
4. I'm not working at the moment.
5. That didn't really happen! / ..., did it?
6. I didn't wait. It was late. 7. We didn't want to take a taxi. 8. He doesn't have / hasn't got much talent.

5. Fragen und Frageanhängsel

32 2. e 3. a 4. b 5. i 6. f 7. c 8. d 9. g

33 1. a 2. b 3. a 4. b

34 2. Do you like 3. Are you taking 4. Did you do 5. should I wear 6. cooked 7. did you ask 8. goes shopping

▶ *Who* ist Subjekt des Fragesatzes: keine Umschreibung mit *do*. *Who* ist Objekt: Umschreibung.

35 Richtig: 2. a 3. b 4. a 5. a 6. a

36 2. e 3. a 4. b 5. d 6. c 7. f 8. g

37 2. Can anyone 3. Were you 4. did you hear 5. did you get 6. Does he know 7. have you been 8. did you do 9. did you do

38 2. are 3. did you interview 4. came 5. interests 6. do people like 7. phoned 8. did you inform 9. were you 10. were you sitting

39 2. do you do 3. do you work 4. Have you been 5. Is it 6. Did you have to 7. Are you 8. Do you have 9. Have you always lived

40 2. f 3. a 4. b 5. h 6. c 7. d 8. e

41 2. aren't we 3. did it 4. won't you 5. was he 6. doesn't she 7. don't you

▶ Bejahter Satz – verneintes Anhängsel (ggfs. *don't / doesn't / didn't* ergänzen). Verneinter Satz – bejahtes Anhängsel.

42 3. Don't you? 4. Does she? 5. Do you? 6. Do they? 7. Did you? 8. Didn't it?

▶ „Echo-Fragen": Bejahter Satz – bejahte Frage. Verneinter Satz – verneinte Frage. In beiden Fällen ggfs. *do(n't) / does(n't) / did(n't)* ergänzen.

6. Zukunftsformen

43 2. I'll give you a hand. 3. I'll lend you the money. 4. I'll give you a lift. 5. I'll get Simon for you. 6. He'll call you back. 7. I'll see if she's here. 8. They'll let you know

▶ Bei spontanen Entscheidungen, Angeboten und Zusagen: *will*

44 2. I'll take 3. I'll have 4. I'll have 5. we'll try 6. we'll take 7. I won't have 8. We'll have

45 2. a 3. b 4. b 5. b 6. b

▶ Gegenwartsformen, um die Zukunft auszudrücken, sind im Englischen seltener als im Deutschen. Unterschiede zwischen den Zukunftsformen:

- *will:* neutrale Form, ohne Färbung durch Absicht, Plan o.ä. (Beachten Sie: „will" = *want to*)
- *going to:* Es besteht die Absicht, etwas zu tun; oder die Gewissheit, dass etwas passieren wird.
- Verlaufsform der Gegenwart: Etwas ist geplant, vorgesehen, abgemacht.
- Einfache Gegenwart: Etwas ist bestimmt durch Fahr- oder Ablaufplan.
- Verlaufsform der *will*-Zukunft: Etwas ist so vorgesehen, wird sich so ergeben.

46 1. a, b, c 2. b, c 3. a, c, d 4. a, b, d

47 1. will only be / is only going to be 2. won't be / isn't going to be 3. are moving / are going to move / will be moving 4. will be lying 5. will have done 6. are you taking / do you take / are you going to take / will you take / will you be taking 7. you'll have / you'll be having / you're having / you're going to have 8. won't be / isn't going to be 9. will have left

▶ Vollendete Zukunft (Nr. 5, 9): *will have* + Partizip Perfekt

7. Aktiv und Passiv

48 2. a series of children's books by J.K. Rowling 3. a film by Steven Spielberg 4. a play by William Shakespeare 5. It is held by Margaret Court. 6. It is held by Michael Schumacher.

49 2. f 3. a 4. g 5. c 6. e 7. h 8. b

50 2. a 3. a 4. b 5. a 6. a 7. a 8. b 9. b 10. b

51 2. will be told 3. is still being tested 4. weren't invited 5. was being filmed 6. is being re-printed 7. was eaten up 8. had not been expected 9. are being monitored

52 2. When was the hotel opened? 3. When will the bags / suitcases be collected? 4. Where were the tickets issued? 5. How were you informed? 6. Will the letterbox / postbox be emptied today? 7. Why haven't the beds been made? 8. Has our order been forgotten? 9. Is a tip expected?

53 1. a + b 2. a. 3. a + b 4. b 5. a + b 6. a 7. a

▶ Bei vielen englischen Verben kann das indirekte Objekt eines Aktivsatzes zum Subjekt eines Passivsatzes gemacht werden. Ausnahmen: *explain, suggest, describe.*

54 2. has the key been deposited 3. will the workforce be informed by 4. is the event being sponsored by 5. was the letter signed by 6. has the company been taken over by 7. was it invented by 8. is the company going to be bailed out by

8. Infinitiv und Gerundium

55 2. a 3. a 4. b 5. a 6. b 7. a 8. b 9. a 10. a 11. b

▶ In *look forward to* ist *to* Präposition, deshalb folgt ein Gerundium.

56 1. trying out / to try out 2. making, doing, doing 3. doing, to make 4. to ask, to remember 5. worrying, (in) getting, worrying 6. enjoying, staying, to do

57 2. I offered to give them a lift. 3. Don't mention meeting me at the café. 4. I admit being there. 5. I really dislike asking for help. 6. We can't carry on meeting like this. 7. They discussed closing the factory in Poland. 8. He claims to have known nothing about it.

58 2. Would you like us to wait 3. I'd like you to go 4. I want you to 5. Does he really expect me to work 6. I need you to pick up 7. Would you like me to shut 8. Do you want me to take 9. I'd love him to make

59 2. b 3. a 4. b 5. a 6. a 7. a 8. a

60 2. h 3. a 4. f 5. b 6. c 7. d 8. g

61 2. Let's take a taxi instead of going on the bus. 3. I asked the question without even thinking. 4. You can improve your vocabulary by reading a lot. 5. Before opening the attachment, scan it for viruses. 6. We drove all the way without stopping. 7. Instead of having coffee I'll take tea for a change. 8. He lost a lot of money by investing in the stock market.

62 2. in 3. at 4. of 5. of 6. in 7. for 8. for 9. on 10. in

63 2. a 3. b 4. a 5. a 6. a 7. a 8. a

▶ *remember/forget:* für Vergangenes: *-ing*-Form; für Zukünftiges: Infinitiv (jeweils vom Erzählzeitpunkt aus gesehen).
stop (aufhören) und *mean* (bedeuten): *-ing*-Form;
stop (anhalten) und *mean* (vorhaben): Infinitiv.

9. *if*-Sätze

64 2. if 3. when 4. If 5. If 6. When 7. if 8. If 9. If

65 1. a 2. b 3. b 4. b

66 2. d 3. g 4. b 5. c 6. e 7. a 8. h 9. i

67 2. If you want, I can 3. If I had seen you, I would have stopped. 4. It would make me ... if I was 5. If it hadn't been cheaper, I wouldn't have bought it. 6. Where would you live if you could choose? 7. They wouldn't have invited me ... if Hannah hadn't said 8. We would fly ... if we had

68 2. will be 3. wouldn't have been 4. didn't drink 5. calls 6. would you have done 7. had 8. could 9. had 10. hadn't seen, wouldn't have believed 11. hadn't gone, would never have met 12. hadn't read, wouldn't have understood

69 1. If the bus doesn't come soon, I'll walk. 2. I wouldn't have said yes if I had been in doubt. 3. I would help you if I knew how (to). 4. If he calls me Fritzi again, I'll kill him. 5. If we had lost, it wouldn't have been the end of the world. 6. It would be terrible if we could control the weather. 7. Even if they gave it (to) me, I wouldn't want it. 8. If I had taken the right clothing/ clothes with me, I wouldn't have frozen all week. 9. If the firm/ company hadn't made these risky investments, it wouldn't have gone bankrupt.

10. Modalverben

70 2. e 3. i 4. a 5. c 6. h 7. b 8. f 9. d

71 2. Shall 3. might not 4. mustn't 5. couldn't 6. Would 7. will

72 1. mustn't 2. needn't 3. mustn't 4. needn't 5. needn't 6. needn't

▶ *mustn't* = nicht dürfen; *needn't* = nicht müssen.

73 1. speak 2. do

74 2. won't be able to 3. haven't been able to 4. weren't able to 5. wasn't able to 6. could have 8. had to 9. will have to 10. won't have to

75 2. do we have to 3. do we have to 4. did you have to 5. doesn't have to 6. didn't have to 7. did you have to 8. won't you have to

76 1. a + b + c 2. c 3. a 4. a 5. b + c

77 1. may / might 2. may / might 3. may / might 4. Were they able to 5. Did you have to 6. have had to 7. mustn't 8. may / might

78 2. b 3. a 4. b 5. a

11. Artikel und Begleiter

79 2. e 3. a 4. c 5. b 6. d

80 2. four times a day 3. twice a week 4. once in a lifetime

81 2. a 3. b 4. a 5. b 6. a 7. a 8. a

82 2. c 3. a 4. b 5. f 6. e

83 2. It was such a terrible journey. 3. What kind/sort of car does he drive? 4. What glorious weather! 5. We meet once a month.

84 2. b 3. b 4. a 5. a 6. a 7. b 8. a

85 2. the 3. the 4. - 5. - 6. - 7. - 8. - 9. - 10. the

86 1. Tim is a friend of mine. 2. Andrea is a colleague of Julia's. 3. A brother of Jack's drives an old Jaguar. 4. Neighbours of ours have a house in Spain.

87 2. democracy 3. The history 4. American history 5. Life, death 6. the death 7. Life 8. time 9. freedom 10. nature

88 1. b 2. c 3. a + b 4. a + b 5. b

12. Singular und Plural

89 2. businesses 3. addresses 4. copies 5. tomatoes, ones 6. brothers-in-law 7. series 8. wolves 9. foxes, mice, sheep 10. teeth

90 2. b 3. a 4. a 5. a 6. b 7. a 8. b 9. a 10. a

91 2. are the police 3. pairs of trousers 4. has 5. is 6. The scissors are 7. The goods are 8. The news is 9. The stairs are

13. Adjektiv und Adverb

92 2. a 3. b 4. a 5. b 6. b 7. a 8. a 9. b 10. b

93 2. g 3. a 4. e 5. b 6. d 7. h 8. f

94 2. well (einziges ohne -*ly*) 3. happy (einziges, das nicht als Adjektiv und Adverb die gleiche Form hat) 4. publicly (einziges, das nicht auf -*ically* endet)

95 2. careful 3. excited 4. excitedly 5. particular 6. particularly 7. lovely 8. lovely 9. Anxious 10. anxious

96 2. well informed 3. hard 4. tragically 5. well developed 6. korrekt 7. well behaved 8. korrekt

97 1. worse 2. lower 3. easier 4. better 5. least 6. more expensive than 7. sooner than 8. more surprised than me / than I am 9. as me / as I have 10. easiest

98 2. b 3. a 4. b 5. a 6. a 7. b 8. b 9. b 10. a

99 2. b 3. a 4. a 5. a 6. a 7. a 8. a

100 1. I take my medicine every day.
2. I'll probably see you again soon.
3. I'll never buy such an old car again!
4. She left the office ten minutes ago.

14. Präpositionen

101 1. b 2. b 3. a 4. a 5. b 6. a 7. a 8. b

102 2. at 3. at / in 4. at 5. At / *(AE:)* On 6. in 7. at 8. on 9. at 10. at 11. on 12. in 13. at 14. at 15. on

103 1. after 2. on 3. at 4. at 5. on 6. in 7. since 8. at 9. on 10. at 11. by 12. on 13. at 14. at 15. for

104 1. a 2. b 3. a

105 2. korrekt 3. during the meeting 4. several years ago 5. by Tuesday 6. korrekt 7. korrekt 8. near

106 1. a 2. a 3. a 4. b 5. b 6. b 7. b 8. a

107 2. except 3. of 4. on 5. on 6. to 7. about 8. besides 9. above 10. at

108 2. at 3. for 4. with 5. in

109 1. a 2. c 3. c 4. b 5. c 6. d 7. c 8. b

15. Dies und das

110 1. a + b + d 2. b 3. d

111 1. a 2. a 3. b 4. b

112 2. they wouldn't have time 3. she was leaving / would be leaving the next day 4. to take a seat 5. if/ whether Rebecca had been invited 6. if I spoke / speak Portuguese 7. he was so excited 8. they weren't expecting us 9. he had made a mistake 10. if/whether James would be there

113 1. a 2. a 3. c 4. a 5. a 6. b 7. c

114 1. b 2. b 3. a 4. a 5. b 6. a

16. True friends?

115 2. e 3. b 4. a 5. d 6. take 7. bring

▶ herbringen = *bring*;
hin-, wegbringen = *take*

116 2. got 3. took 4. take 5. bring 6. put

> ▶ siehe 115

117 2. c 3. d 4. c 5. c 6. c 7. d 8. b 9. b

> ▶ herkommen = *come;* hinkommen = *get;* hingehören = *go;* kommen lassen = *send for*

118 1. map 2. menu 3. tickets 4. card 5. ticket

> ▶ Landkarte = *map;* Speisekarte = *menu;* Eintritts-, Fahrkarte = *ticket;* Karte zum Schreiben = *card*

119 1. to walk 2. last 3. go to school 4. isn't working 5. is your flight / does your plane go / does your flight go 6. run 7. That's impossible

> ▶ gehen (allgemein) = *go*; zu Fuß gehen = walk; verkehren = *run, go*; funktionieren = *work;* (an)dauern = *last*

120 1. a 2. b 3. a 4. b 5. b

> ▶ aus dem Gedächtnis verlieren = *forget*; liegen lassen + Ortsbestimmung = *leave*

121 1. a wine glass 2. a glass of wine 3. a jar of olives 4. a jar of honey

> ▶ Glas (Material, Trinkgefäß, Getränk) = *glass*; Glas (Aufbewahrungsgefäß mit Deckel) = *jar*

122 1. salad 2. gravy 3. dressing 4. sauce 5. lettuce

> ▶ Salat (als Gericht/Beilage) = *salad;* Salat (als Pflanze/Blätter) = *lettuce;* Bratensoße = *gravy;* Salatsoße = *dressing;* Schokoladensoße = *chocolate sauce*

123 1. sharp 2. hot/spicy

> ▶ scharf (Messer, Frost) = *sharp;* scharf (Essen) = *spicy/hot*

124 1. guest 2. host 3. guest 4. customers 5. guest 6. visitor 7. passenger 8. inn 9. guesthouse

125 1. korrekt 2. studying/revising 3. korrekt

> ▶ lernen (generell) = *learn;* für die Schule lernen, wiederholen = *study / revise*

126 1. false 2. wrong 3. false 4. wrong 5. false 6. wrong 7. wrong 8. wrong 9. wrong 10. false

> ▶ unwahr, unecht = *false;* fehlerhaft, nicht korrekt = *wrong*

127 1. have/take a coffee break 2. There was a short pause 3. The play was very long and there were two intervals/intermissions. 4. On some days I have so much to do that I don't take/have a lunch break. 5. Break is after the second lesson.

> ▶ kurze Unterbrechung = *pause;* längere Unterbrechung, Erholungspause = *break;* Pause bei Konzerten o. a. = *interval / intermission*

128 1. b 2. a, b 3. a 4. a 5. a 6. a 7. a

▶ bei Sachen mit überdurchschnittlichem Durchmesser = *thick;* bei Personen = *fat;* bei Geld o.a. (üppig) = *big fat;* bei Fehlern = *big;* bei Freunden (eng, vertraut) = *close*

129 1. Does that cost extra?
2. I'll pay for the wine separately.
3. I bought the wine specially for you.
4. He did it on purpose, I'm sure.

▶ zusätzlich = *extra;* gesondert = *separately;* speziell = *specially;* absichtlich = *on purpose*

130 1. (for) a long time 2. For twenty years 3. length 4. length 5. a long time

▶ *long* i.d.R. nur in Fragen und verneinten Sätzen, sonst *a long time*

131 1. b 2. a

▶ Preis, den man zahlt = *price;* Preis, den man gewinnt = *prize*

132 1. Have you heard / Did you hear 2. listening 3. listened to 4. hear 5. listen 6. Listen, hear

▶ hören (akustisch wahrnehmen) = *hear;* hören (Radio, Musik) = *listen to;* zuhören, sich anhören, auf jmdn./etw. hören = *listen to*

133 1. tell 2. tell 3. say 4. Say 5. tell 6. Tell

▶ angesprochene Person wird nicht genannt = *say;* sie wird genannt = *tell.* Ausnahmen: *tell a story* (eine Geschichte erzählen), *tell the truth* (die Wahrheit sagen), *tell lies* (lügen).

134 1. Can you tell me what it costs / will cost? 2. I always tell the truth. 3. She said *Happy birthday,* but it wasn't my birthday. 4. She's a very quiet person. She doesn't say much. 5. What did he tell you / say to you? 6. What did he say?
7. He said he couldn't tell us anything.
8. The match was boring. – You can say that again!

▶ siehe 133

135 1. control 2. check 3. control 4. control 5. checked 6. checked 7. checks

▶ unter Kontrolle haben, steuern = *control;* kontrollieren (überprüfen, ob etw. in Ordnung ist, z.B. Fahrkarten, Sicherheit) = *check*

136 1. make 6. cuisine/food 7. is boiling

▶ Essen zubereiten im Allgemeinen = *cook;* Tee, Kaffee, Suppe zubereiten = *make*; sieden = *boil*

137 1. warm 2. hot 3. hot 4. hot 5. hot 6. hot/warm

▶ angenehm warm = *warm;* unangenehm warm = *hot; warm* (bei Wasser, Essen) = *hot*

138 1. fresh 2. chilly 3. clean 4. bright 5. Wet

139 1. nil nil 2. zero 3. nought/zero/oh 4. oh/zero 5. zero

▶ beim Sport = *nil;* bei Temperaturangaben = *zero;* in Dezimalzahlen = *nought, zero;* in Telefon- und Kontonummern = *oh, zero*

140 1. latest 2. new 3. latest 4. nearest 5. Next

▶ nächste(r/s) (räumlich am nächsten) = *nearest;* nächste(r/s) (zeitlich/räumlich nächstfolgend) = *next;* neueste(r/s) (aktuellste[r/s]) = *latest*

141 1. b 2. a

▶ Motor eines kleineren Geräts = *motor;* Motor (bei Auto, Bus usw.) = *engine*

142 1. technique 2. technology 3. technique 4. technology

▶ Methode, Arbeitsweise = *technique;* Wissenschaft, Technologie = *technology*

143 1. shade 2. shadows 3. shadow 4. shadow 5. shade

▶ schattiger Platz = *shade;* Schattenumriss = *shadow*

144 1. b 2. a 3. a 4. a,b 5. a 6. a 7. a, b 8. b

▶ schlafen (allgemein) = *sleep;* schlafen (im Zustand des Schlafens sein) = *be asleep;* ausschlafen, lange schlafen = *sleep in/late*

145 1. politics 2. policy/policies 3. policy/policies

▶ Politik (politisches Leben) = *politics;* Politik (Inhalte, Strategie) = *policy*

146 1. They didn't have satellite TV and there were only three channels. 2. There are a lot of improvements in the new version of the program. 3. The festival programme has now appeared. 4. Which channel do you watch most?

▶ Plan = *programme (GB) / program (AE);* Computerprogramm = *program;* Fernsehkanal = *channel*

147 1. office/building 2. korrekt 3. GP (= general practitioner) 4. home

▶ Wohnhaus = *house;* Gebäude = *building;* Firmenräume = *office*

148 1. korrekt 2. korrekt 3. think 4. korrekt 5. think

▶ sagen wollen = *mean;* glauben = *think*

149 1. point (0.7%) 2. comma

▶ Zeichensetzung im Text = *comma;* in Dezimalzahlen = *point*

150 1. b 2. b 3. b 4. b

▶ wollen (generell) = *want;* im Begriff sein, etwas zu tun = *to be about to do something;* nicht wollen (wenn etwas Erwünschtes nicht eintritt/eintrat) = *won't/wouldn't*

151 1. Who(m) do you want to speak to/with? 2. I was just about to leave when Jim called/phoned. 3. The visitor wants to see Mr Smith. 4. I want to go to bed. 5. she just won't listen 6. I tried to open the window, but it wouldn't. 7. What are you trying to say?! 8. We could go to the theatre if you like/want.

▶ siehe 150

152 1. cost 2. costs 3. cost 4. take 5. expense 6. cost

153 1. It's no use/good. 2. is good for 3. There's only one thing to do

▶ behilflich sein = *help;* helfen gegen (bei Arzneimitteln usw.) = *be good for;* nichts helfen (aussichtslos sein) = *be no use/good*

154 1. richtig 2. falsch (richtig: audience)

▶ publik = *public;* Publikum = *audience*

155 1. open air / countryside 2. human nature 3. nature

▶ natürliche Welt der Pflanzen, Tiere usw. = *nature;* Wesen = *nature;* die freie Natur = *the open air / the countryside*

156 1. if 2. when 3. when 4. If 5. If 6. if 7. if 8. When 9. If

▶ unter der Bedingung, dass ... = *if;* gleichzeitig oder unmittelbar vorzeitig ablaufende Handlungen = *when*

157 1. b, c 2. a, b 3. b

158 1. b 2. a 3. a 4. b

▶ Tat, Handlung = *action;* Werbe-, Spenden-, Militäraktion = *campaign*

159 2. steal 3. steal 4. rob 5. rob 6. rob 7. rob 8. steal 9. steal 10. rob

▶ einer Person/Bank etw. nehmen = *rob;* etw. rauben = *steal*

160 1. It was cold and we had deep snow. 2. Santa Claus lives in the far north. 3. It was high summer and the grass was long. 4. How large was the amount that was stolen? 5. She has a highly paid job with a computer company. 6. The town is surrounded by high mountains. 7. Hands up! 8. The train went into the tunnel at high speed. 9. We're not expecting more than 30 people at the most. 10. More and more people are living to a great age. 11. He has heavy debts. 12. The team won by a long way / by a wide margin.

161 1. c 2. b, c 3. a, b 4. d 5. b 6. b 7. Robin and Ann send their best wishes.

162 1. street 2. road 3. road 4. street

163 1. road 2. streets 3. street 4. roads 5. road 6. road 7. road 8. streets

164 1. d 2. d

▶ Stadion = *stadium;* in diesem Stadium = *at this stage*

165 1. do 2. do 3. do 4. make 5. do 6. make 7. do 8. make 9. do 10. do 11. do 12. make

▶ herstellen, erzeugen, schaffen usw. = *make;* erledigen, sich beschäftigen mit = *do;* machen (in festen Wendungen) = *have, take, go ...*

166 1. When are you having/taking a holiday / going on holiday this year? 2. Wait, I want to take a photo. 3. It doesn't matter. 4. Shall we take/have a break? 5. I'm on a diet. 6. When are you taking your exam? 7. Don't worry.

▶ siehe 165

167 1. is making 2. go 3. go for 4. got 5. make 6. doing 7. make 8. do 9. have 10. done 11. doing

▶ siehe 165

17. False friends

168 1. b, c 2. b

▶ Fabrik = *factory; fabric* = Stoff

169 2. korrekt 3. review

▶ Happy End = *happy ending;* Kritik = *review; critic* = Kritiker/in, Rezensent/in

170 1. form 2. formula 3. Formula 4. formula 5. form

▶ Formular = *form; formula* = Formel

171 1. b, c 2. a, b

▶ überhören = *don't hear, fail to hear; overhear* = (zufällig) mithören

172 2. business 3. takeover 4. overtook 5. staff 6. personal 7. undertaker 8. entrepreneurs 9. boss 10. chef

▶ Branche = *business; branch* = Zweigstelle; Chef = *boss; chef* = Koch, Küchenchef; Personal = *staff; personal* = persönlich; Übernahme = *takeover; overtake* = überholen; Unternehmer = *entrepreneur; undertaker* = Bestattungsunternehmen

173 1. a, b, c 2. b

▶ Rückseite = *back; backside* = Hintern

174 1. self-conscious 2. self-confident 3. sensible 4. sensitive 5. pleasant 6. sympathetic

▶ selbstbewusst = *self-confident; self-conscious* = gehemmt, unsicher; sensibel = *sensitive; sensible* = vernünftig; sympathisch = *pleasant; sympathetic* = mitfühlend

175 1. a, d 2. c

▶ ordinär = *common, vulgar; ordinary* = durchschnittlich, normal

176 1. cake 2. biscuit / cookie

▶ Keks = *biscuit (BE) / cookie (AE); cake* = Kuchen

177 opinion

▶ Meinung = *opinion; meaning* = Bedeutung

178 1. marks/grades 2. notes 3. note 4. note 5. notice 6. notice 7. note 8. music

▶ Note = *mark/grade; note* = Notiz, Zettel; Notiz = *note; notice* = Aushang

179 1. d 2. c

▶ bekommen = *get/have/receive; become* = werden

180 1. When is the courier going to pick up / collect the parcels? 2. ... a package of measures 3. I use several Microsoft software packages. 4. Two packets of butter and a packet of tea.

▶ Paket = *parcel, package; packet* = Päckchen

181 1. korrekt 2. draft 3. plan 4. threw him

▶ Konzept = *plan/draft; concept* = Begriff

182 1. a map 2. a tablet 3. a folder 4. a tray 5. a photograph 6. a photographer

▶ Mappe = *folder; map* = Landkarte; Tablett = *tray; tablet* = Tablette; Fotograf = *photographer; photograph* = Foto

183 1. murder 2. murderer 3. poison 4. gifts

▶ Mörder = *murderer; murder* = Mord; Gift = *poison; gift* = Geschenk

184 1. I paid and the taxi driver gave me a receipt. 2. It tastes wonderful. You must give me the recipe. 3. The prescription still has to be signed by the doctor. 4. What's your recipe for success?

▶ Rezept (beim Arzt) = *prescription;* Rezept (beim Kochen oder als Erfolgsrezept) = *recipe; receipt* = Quittung

185 1. b 2. b, c 3. c

▶ Rente = *pension; rent* = Miete

186 1. valid, up to date 2. topical 3. current

▶ gültig = *valid;* von momentanem Interesse = *topical;* gegenwärtig = *current; actual(ly)* = tatsächlich

187 1. spare 2. save 3. spent 4. donate 5. save

▶ sparen = *save; spare* = entbehren; spenden = *donate; spend* = (Geld) ausgeben; (Zeit) verbringen

188 1. mobile (phone) / cell phone 2. indicated 3. overlooked

▶ übersehen = *overlook; oversee* = beaufsichtigen; Handy = *mobile (phone) (BE) / cell phone (AE); handy* = praktisch, griffbereit; blinken = *indicate; blink* = zwinkern

189 1. c 2. a 3. b, d

▶ Gymnasium = *grammar school; gymnasium* = Turn-, Sporthalle; Mobbing = *bullying; mob* = belagern; brav = *good; brave* = mutig

190 1. Gymnastics 2. exercises 3. wandering 4. hiking

▶ Gymnastik (Wettkampfdisziplin) = *gymnastics;* Gymnastik (private Freiübungen) = *exercises;* wandern = *hike; wander* = ziellos umherstreifen, bummeln

191 1. brochures 2. advertisement 3. prospects 4. announcements

▶ Prospekt = *brochure; prospect* = Aussicht; Annonce = *advertisement; announcement* = Bekanntgabe, Ankündigung

192 1. founded 2. founded 3. grounded

▶ gründen = *found; ground* = Startverbot erhalten (bei Flugzeugen)

193 1. at last, finally 2. sometime, one day

▶ *eventually* = schließlich, endlich

194 1. a, b, c 2. b, c, d

▶ eventuell = *may ..., ... possibly ..., (it's) possible ...*

195 1. material / fabric 2. material / fabric 3. substances 4. material

▶ Stoff (Gewebe) = *material / fabric;* Stoff (natürlicher Bestandteil) = *substance;* Stoff (Handlung) = *material; stuff* = Zeug

196 1. d 2. a

▶ Warenhaus = *department store; warehouse* = Lager(haus)

197 1. denomination 2. confession

▶ Konfession = *denomination; confession* = Beichte

198 1. engaged 2. dedicated 3. committed 4. involved 5. active 6. hired

▶ engagiert = *involved, dedicated, committed; engaged* = verlobt

18. Lots of friends

199 1. husband 2. man 3. woman 4. wife 5. Goodness! / Oh boy! / Wow!

▶ Frau / Mann (weiblicher / männlicher Mensch) = *man / woman*; Ehefrau / -mann = *wife / husband*

200 2. c 3. a 4. e 5. d

▶ in Bitten, Fragen = *please;* Reaktion auf Dank = *not at all / that's OK / it's a pleasure ...;* Reaktion auf Entschuldigung = *it's/that's all right / never mind*; Zustimmung zu einer Bitte = *certainly / of course / please do;* wie bitte? = *sorry? excuse me? pardon?;* beim Überreichen = *here you are.*

201 1. Certainly. / Of course. / Please do. 2. Here you are. 3. Sorry? / Pardon? / Excuse me? 4. please 5. It's a pleasure. / That's all right. / You're welcome.

▶ siehe 200

202 1. When 2. than 3. as 4. As

▶ zeitlich = *when;* bei Komparativen = *than;* „genau wie" = *as;* als (ob) = *as (if);* in der Eigenschaft als ... = *as*

203 1. visit 2. attend / go to 3. go to

▶ besuchen (als Gast, Tourist usw.) = *visit;* besuchen (Schule, Kirche usw.) = *attend/go to;* besuchen (kulturelle Veranstaltungen) = *go to*

204 2. pay for 3. pay 4. pay for 5. pay 6. pay 7. pay for 8. pay 9. pay 10. pay for

▶ bei Produkten und Dienstleistungen = *pay for;* bei Personen, Beträgen, Rechnungen = *pay*

205 2. remember 3. memories 4. short-term memory 5. remember 6. remind 7. reminder 8. remembers

▶ sich erinnern = *remember;* jmdn. erinnern = *remind somebody;* Erinnerung (im Gedächtnis) = *memory;* Erinnerung (Gedächtnisstütze) = *reminder;* Gedächtnis = *memory*

206 Across: 3. fit 5. well 6. good for you
Down: 1. better 2. healthy 4. common

▶ in guter körperlicher Verfassung = *healthy / fit;* genesen = *better;* gesundheitsfördernd = *good for you*

207 1. b 2. c 3. c 4. c 5. a 6. b 7. a 8. b 9. b 10. b 11. a

▶ fahren (ganz allgemein) = *go;* bei Auto = *drive;* bei Fahrrad und Motorrad = *ride;* mit Geschwindigkeitsangabe = *do / travel at;* im Sinne von „verkehren" = *run;* fahren mit Verkehrsmitteln = *take*

208 1. instructor 2. teacher 3. instructor 4. instructor 5. teacher 6. instructors 7. teachers

▶ Lehrer für Kopfarbeit = *teacher;* Lehrer für praktische Fertigkeiten = *instructor*

209 1. tight 2. close 3. narrow 4. closely

▶ schmal = *narrow;* eng anliegend, stramm = *tight;* nahe, vertraut = *close;* als Adverb = *closely*

210 1. about 2. for 3. around/about 4. to 5. to 6. into 7. for

▶ etw. dagegen tun = *do something about;* als Schutz gegen etw. = *for;* zeitlich = *around / about;* bei Widerstand o.a. = *to;* bei Austausch = *for*

211 1. a 2. a 3. a 4. b 5. b

▶ als Schauspieler auftreten = *act;* aufführen = *perform;* sich abspielen = *to be set;* (eine Rolle) spielen = *play*

212 1. tall 2. big/great 3. great 4. big/great 5. large 6. big 7. great 8. big 9. great 10. big/large 11. big/great 12. great

▶ bei Sachen = *big;* bei Menschen = *tall;* im Sinne von kräftig, älter = *big;* beträchlich = *big, great* (bei Nomen ohne Plural nur *great* möglich); berühmt, bedeutend = *great;* umsatzstark, erfolgreich = *big;* bei Mengen, Dimensionen = *large*

213 1. smaller 2. little 3. little 4. small 5. small 6. small 7. small 8. small 9. little 10. little

▶ als neutraler Ausdruck = *small;* emotional gefärbt (niedlich / schrecklich klein) = *little;* jünger = *little*

214 1. hear 2. understand 3. hear

▶ begreifen = *understand;* akustisch wahrnehmen = *hear*

215 Across: 1. stay 3. remains 4. stopped
Down: 1. standing 2. keep

▶ im gleichen Zustand bleiben = *stay, keep;* am gleichen Ort bleiben = *stay;* übrig bleiben = *remain;* stehenbleiben (nicht mehr gehen) = *stop*

216 1. fast 2. quick 3. fast 4. quick 5. fast 6. quickly

▶ schnell (von der Bewegung her) = *fast;* schnell (nur kurze Zeit beanspruchend) = *quick*

217 1. room 2. square 3. is this seat taken 4. courts 5. course 6. sports ground 7. place 8. have a seat 9. place 10. room

▶ Ort, Stelle, Studienplatz = *place;* ausreichend Raum = *room, space;* in einer Stadt = *square;* beim Tennis = *court;* beim Golf = *course;* Sitzplatz = *seat*

218 1. drive / journey / trip 2. weekend trip 3. ten-minute bus ride 4. travel 5. tour 6. car journeys

▶ Reise generell (meist mit Aufenthalt am Zielort) = *trip;* Autofahrt = *drive;* längere Fahrt ohne Aufenthalt = *journey;* das Reisen = *travel;* Rundreise = *tour*

219 1. How long does it take from here to Strasbourg? 2. It takes about four hours by car. 3. It took me two whole days to get my presentation ready. 4. I know. That sort of thing takes a lot of time.

▶ brauchen (Zeit) = *take*

220 1. I need your help. It will only take a few minutes. 2. You don't need to / You needn't wait for me. 3. By train it takes one and a half hours. 4. The journey takes one and a half hours. 5. The film lasts 30 minutes. 6. You don't need to / You needn't bring anything with you, we have everything. 7. I need another two hours. This sort of job/work takes a long time.

▶ etw./jmdn. benötigen = *need;* brauchen nicht zu ... = *don't need to / needn't;* brauchen (Zeit) = *take/last*

221 1. b 2. b 3. b 4. a 5. b 6. b 7. b 8. a 9. a 10. b 11. b 12. b 13. b 14. b 15. b 16. a

▶ mit Hand / Körperteil halten = *hold;* in einem Zustand belassen = *keep;* jmdn. festhalten = *stop;* bei Versprechen = *keep;* bei Rede = *make, give;* jmdn. für etw. ansehen = *think of someone as something;* sich halten an = *stick to;* (an)dauern = *last*

222 1. suit 2. suit 3. fit 4. fit 5. match

▶ passen (Größe, Dimensionen) = *fit;* gut stehen = *suit;* passen (zu etw. anderem) = *match;* recht sein = *suit*

223 1. a, c 2. d 3. a, c, d 4. c 5. a, b

▶ studieren = *be a student, be at / go to university;* Studium = *subject, (university/degree) course*

224 1. with 2. at 3. With 4. near 5. for/with 6. at/on 7. over 8. at 9. in 10. on/with 11. at 12. at 13. with

▶ bei jdm zu Hause = *with someone / at someone's house;* in der Nähe von = *near;* bei Firma = *for;* bei Bedingungen = *at*

225 1. job 2. work 3. work 4. job 5. job 6. job

▶ Arbeit (allgemein oder als Arbeitsort) = *work;* einzelne, bestimmte Arbeit, Anstellung = *job*
Beachten Sie: *work* kann nicht mit dem unbestimmten Artikel stehen.

226 1. recognized 2. realized/recognized 3. realized 4. realized 5. recognized

▶ mit den Sinnen wiedererkennen = *recognize;* geistig entdecken = *realize;* politisch = *recognize*

227 Across: 1. eventually 3. finally 4. after all
Down: 1. end 2. at last

▶ als Folge, am Schluss = *eventually, in the end;* später als erwartet bzw. gewünscht = *finally;* schließlich doch, richtig betrachtet = *after all;* endlich nach langem Ersehnen = *at last*

228 1. light 2. slight 3. easy 4. a slight 5. A light 6. I found it easy

▶ einfach = *easy;* geringfügig = *slight;* von geringem Gewicht = *light*

229 1. by 2. of 3. out of 4. of mine 5. by 6. of

▶ bei Urhebern = *by*

230 1. c 2. a, c 3. b, c 4. a 5. c 6. c 7. b, c 8. a 9. c 10. b, c 11. b 12. b, c

▶ schwer (von Gewicht) = *heavy;* schwierig = *difficult, hard;* ernsthaft = *serious*

231 1. b 2. c 3. a 4. c

232 1. bad 2. poor 3. off 4. sick 5. poorly

▶ negativ = *bad;* sich schlecht (krank) fühlen = *feel sick;* bei Qualität = *poor;* bei Lebensmitteln = *off*

233 1. Everybody / Everyone thinks the same.
2. I'm prepared/willing to do anything to help you.
3. Every two or three days I get an email.
4. My motto is: All or nothing.
5. We all need a break.
6. Everybody / Everyone was enthusiastic.

234 2. b 3. a 4. b 5. a 6. a 7. b 8. b 9. b 10. b

▶ bis (+ zeitlicher Endpunkt) = *till / until;* bis spätestens = *by;* bei Mengen-/Zahlenangaben = *up to;* räumlich = *as far as / to*

235 1. the same age 2. the same size 3. the same clothes

▶ gleich + bestimmtes Adjektiv = *the same* + Nomen

236 1. Have you finished? 2. Are you ready for dessert?

▶ bereit = *ready;* erledigt, abgeschossen = *finished*

237 1. c, speak 2. a, at 3. e, do 4. b, get on 5. f, could 6. d, go/carry

238 1. be / become 2. go 3. are turning 4. is becoming / is getting 5. grow 6. has turned out 7. got 8. is going

▶ Berufspläne = *be / become;* Zustandsveränderung = *get / become;* Negativveränderung = *go;* allmähliche Veränderung = *grow;* Farbveränderung = *turn / go*

239 1. realize 2. note 3. noticed

▶ sich geistig bewusst werden = *realize;* mit den Sinnen wahrnehmen = *notice;* sich merken = *note, remember*

240 1. recently/lately 2. At the beginning 3. in the next (few) weeks/months

241 1. Have you ever been to Mexico?
2. I've been to New York before.
3. I would like to visit Ireland sometime.
4. Listen carefully because I'm only going to say it once.
5. Once upon a time there was a king.
6. The town was once famous.

242 1. ex-husband 2. a previous marriage 3. used to live 4. sooner 5. once 6. previous 7. former 8. a previous 9. once 10. used to meet

▶ vorhergehend = *previous;* ehemalig = *former / ex;* früher (eher) = *earlier / sooner;* früher einmal = *once;* früher habe / bin ich immer ... = *I used to ...*

243 1. he's having 2. it says 3. suits 4. stand 5. is complete/finished

244 1. b 2. b 3. a 4. b

▶ während (Konjunktion) = *while;* während (Präposition vor Nomen) = *during*

245 1. strong 2. heavy 3. heavily 4. hard 5. great 6. heavy 7. badly 8. strong 9. heavily 10. 600-page long

▶ bei Regen, Rauchen, Verkehr = *heavy*

246 Across: 4. outside 5. in front of
Down: 1. ago 2. with 3. before 6. to

▶ räumlich = *in front of/outside;* zeitlich (Gegenteil von „nach") = *before;* zeitlich (im Sinne von „her") = *ago;* bei Uhrzeit = *to*

247 1. quiet 2. calm 3. calm 4. quiet 5. still

▶ leise, unauffällig, schweigsam = *quiet;* ruhig, gelassen, reglos = *calm / still* (Sitzen)

248 1. How are things? Everything OK?
2. What was the weather like?
3. What's the new boss like?
4. How do you say that in English?
5. He's not as old as her.
6. What's the phone number?
7. What was it like travelling alone?
8. It's a building like a hotel.

249 1. even 2. Me too 3. So do I 4. Neither will we 5. either 6. Even if 7. so

250 1. aware / conscious 2. aware
3. consciously 4. conscious
5. conscious

▶ um etw. wissend = *aware / conscious* (bei „as far as ..." nur *aware* möglich, vor Nomen nur *conscious* möglich); wissentlich = *conscious(ly)*; ...-bewusst = *...-conscious*

251 1. The police wanted to see my driving licence (BE) / driver's license (AE).
2. Our son has just started taking driving lessons.
3. Our daughter has already passed her (driving) test. / Our daughter already has a driving licence / driver's license.

252 1. wear 2. carry 3. supported
4. carry 5. bear 6. bears 7. wear
8. bear 9. wear

▶ befördern = *carry;* am Körper anhaben = *wear;* im übertragenen Sinne = *bear*

253 1. a 2. a 3. a 4. c 5. a 6. b 7. c
8. b 9. a 10. b 11. a 12. a, b, c
13. b, c 14. b 15. b

▶ räumlich = *above/over;* betreffend = *about;* auf dem Wege = *via;* bei Zahlenangaben = *over*

254 1. nein 2. ja 3. nein 4. ja 5. ja
6. nein 7. ja 8. ja 9. nein 10. ja

2. It's already half past two.
4. Has Tony phoned yet?
5. Even before he got/stood up, I knew what he would say.
7. Have you ever been to Disneyland? / Have you been to Disneyland before?
8. The first guests are already here / have already arrived.
10. Very soon we shall/will hear the first results.

19. Confusing friends

255 1. advice 2. advise

▶ *advice* = Rat(schlag) (Nomen); *advise* = (be)raten (Verb)

256 1. b 2. a

▶ *homework* = Hausaufgabe(n); *housework* = Haushaltsarbeit(en)

257 1. a 2. b 3. a

▶ *interesting* = interessant; *interested* = interessiert

258 1. Is the Sahara the largest desert in the world? 2. What would you like for dessert?

▶ *desert* = Wüste; *dessert* = Dessert

259 1. economic 2. economic
3. economical 4. economic
5. economical 6. economical

▶ *economic* = die Wirtschaft betreffend; *economical* = sparsam

260 1. classical 2. korrekt 3. classical 4. korrekt 5. korrekt 6. classical

▶ *classic* = angesehen, typisch, zeitlos; *classical* = klassisch (in Bezug auf Musik, die Antike)

261 1. beside 2. besides 3. besides 4. besides 5. Besides working 6. beside

▶ *beside* = (örtlich) neben; *besides* = neben (= außer), außerdem

262 1. It's 2. its 3. its 4. its 5. It's 6. its

▶ *it's* = es ist (= it is); *its* = sein, ihr

263 1. altogether 2. all together

▶ *altogether* = insgesamt; *all together* = alle zusammen

264 1. lie 2. lays 3. lain 4. lied 5. lying 6. laid 7. lying 8. lay 9. laid, laid 10. lay, lain 11. lied, lied

265 1. largely 2. largely 3. greatly 4. greatly

▶ *largely* = größtenteils; *greatly* = sehr

266 1. passed 2. past 3. passed 4. past 5. past 6. past 7. past 8. passed

▶ *passed* = Form des Verbs *pass* (vergehen, überholen, vorbeigehen an); *past* = Präposition / Adverb (an … vorbei, vorbei)

267 1. a 2. b

▶ *terrible* = furchtbar; *terrific* = gewaltig, toll

268 1. used to work 2. had to get used to writing 3. get used to it 4. am used to using

▶ *used to* (+ Verb in Grundform) = früher + Verb in der Vergangenheit; *be used to* (+ *-ing*-Form) = es gewohnt sein, zu …; *get used to* = sich gewöhnen an

269 1. at last 2. at least

270 1. risen 2. raised 3. raised 4. rose 5. rose 6. raise

▶ *raise, raised, raised* = an-, auf-, hochheben; *rise, rose, risen* = steigen, an-, auf-, hochsteigen, sich erheben

271 1. a 2. b

▶ *sometime* = irgendwann; *sometimes* = manchmal

272 1. a 2. b

▶ *every day* = jeden Tag; *everyday* = alltäglich

273 1. historic 2. historical 3. historical 4. historical

▶ *historic* = historisch (= bedeutsam); *historical* = geschichtlich, aus der Geschichte

274 1. b 2. a

▶ *affect* = beeinflussen, betreffen (Verb); *effect* = Auswirkung (Nomen)

275 1. loose 2. lose 3. lose 4. loose

▶ *loose* = lose; *lose* = verlieren

276 1. mayor 2. major

▶ *major* = Major; *mayor* = Bürgermeister

277 1. b 2. b 3. a

▶ *in time* = rechtzeitig; *on time* = pünktlich

20. All friends together

278 1. I'll have 2. menu 3. cuisine / food 4. mobile (phone) (BE) / cell phone (AE) 5. inn/pub 6. opinion

279 1. play/piece 2. audience 3. interval 4. poorly attended

280 1. commercial 2. channels 3. newsreaders 4. latest

281 1. a 2. b 3. b 4. b 5. a 6. a

282 1. trays 2. menu 3. salad bar 4. good for you 5. salad dressing

283 1. answer it 2. code 3. take the call 4. ask for 5. dial 6. hung up

284 1. reunion 2. grammar school 3. at 4. marks/grades 5. did/took 6. bullied 7. took/passed 8. went to/ started university

285 1. did / went on 2. stay 3. guesthouses 4. hot 5. took 6. It took us 7. checked 8. forms 9. Altogether

286 1. sleep in 2. ride 3. used to drive 4. two years ago 5. took 6. hard 7. road 8. the open air 9. hiking 10. photographer 11. am also interested in 12. classic 13. are set in

287 1. lately/recently 2. three months 3. latest 4. At this stage 5. current 6. during/over 7. take 8. does it take 9. than

288 1. I like Ronaldo's wife a lot. / Ronaldo's wife is very nice.
2. Anna is very self-confident.
3. Mark is my son from my / a previous marriage.
4. I'm the same age as my boss.
5. Be careful. He's very sensitive.
6. Please leave me alone / in peace. I have to (do some) work.
7. My riding instructor is very tall, almost/ nearly two metres tall.
8. Be sensible!
9. Why are you so quiet today?
10. When was the last time we were all together?
11. My husband is one of the few men who are not interested in football.
12. The children were very good / well behaved.

289 1. Surgery hours 2. good for you 3. prescription 4. painkillers 5. false teeth 6. a really bad sore throat

290 1. next 2. nearest 3. shade 4. shadow 5. backside 6. back

291 1. lettuce 2. boiled potatoes 3. hot/spicy 4. drinking water 5. tray 6. Bon appétit / Enjoy it 7. makes me/you fat 8. have a barbecue 9. hot 10. leftovers 11. loaf 12. recipe 13. dressing 14. menu 15. break 16. inn

292 1. staff 2. have gone into retirement / have retired 3. do / are doing overtime 4. boss 5. entrepreneur 6. takes/makes

293 1. a 2. c 3. c 4. a 5. b 6. c

Register

Register

Die Zahlen beziehen sich auf die durchnummerierten Übungen.